PREVENTING LITIGATION IN SPECIAL EDUCATION

I D E A

WORKBOOK

A Supplement to The Everyday Guide to Special Education Law

Dr. Jacque Phillips, Esq.
Randy Chapman, Esq.

Preventing Litigation in Special Education Workbook
A Supplement to *The Everyday Guide to Special Education Law*
By Dr. Jacque Phillips, Esq. and Randy Chapman, Esq.

This publication is designed to provide accurate and general information in regard to the subject matter covered. It is sold with the understanding that the authors and the publisher are not engaged in rendering legal or other professional services. If specific legal advice is required, please consult an attorney.

Publisher's Cataloging-In-Publication Data
(Prepared by The Donohue Group, Inc.)

Phillips, Jacque.
  Preventing litigation in special education workbook : a supplement to The everyday guide to special education law / by Jacque Phillips and Randy Chapman.

      p. ; cm.

  Includes index.
  ISBN: 978-0-9770179-4-2

  1. United States. Individuals with Disabilities Education Improvement Act of 2004--Case studies. 2. United States. Individuals with Disabilities Education Act--Case studies. 3. United States. Americans with Disabilities Act of 1990--Case studies. 4. United States. Rehabilitation Act of 1973--Case studies. 5. Special education--Law and legislation--United States--Case studies. 6. Children with disabilities--Education--Law and legislation--United States—Case studies. I. Chapman, Randy. Everyday guide to special education law. II. Title.

KF4209.3 .P54 2011
344.0791

Book and Cover Design by MacGraphics Services
Edited by Mary Anne Harvey
Production coordinated by Julie Z. Busby, Randy Chapman and Mary Anne Harvey
Indexing by Katie Bright, Eagle-Eye Indexing
Printing by United Graphics, Inc.

Table of Contents

Acknowledgements

Dr. Jacque Phillips, Esq.

I would like to acknowledge my mentors in the field of special education law including Randy Chapman, Alison Daniels, Sandra Roesti, Kim Dvorchak, and Professor Hardaway. Many of my university students "test drove" the workbook and gave feedback for which I am grateful. Dr. Sarah DeHaas did primary editing which was critical. I also want to thank the people in my world who have been supportive on this and all my work: Mom, Amanda (and those beautiful babies), Jeff, Jon, Bob and the whole "Pack" in which my family travels.

Randy Chapman, Esq.

I would like to acknowledge Mary Anne Harvey, the Executive Director of The Legal Center for People with Disabilities and Older People, for coordinating the production of this book and for her excellent editing skills. Thanks to Julie Busby, our Office Manager, for her many suggestions and help in the book's production.

I want to express my appreciation for the support of the board members and staff of The Legal Center for People with Disabilities and Older People, past and present. Since the creation of The Legal Center in 1976, their work has made a difference in the lives of people with disabilities and older people.

Last but not least, I want to acknowledge Carol, Connor, and Sean Chapman for letting me live with them.

Dedication

Jacque Phillips dedicates this book
in memory of

Granny Bergan,
for teaching us to travel in "Packs."

Randy Chapman dedicates this book
in memory of

Diane Carabello
who worked tirelessly to help raise funds for The Legal Center for People
with Disabilities and Older People and our publishing endeavor

and

Patricia S. Tomlan, Ph.D.
She was a teacher's teacher and advocate for the rights of children with disabilities.

Introduction

Students with disabilities are entitled to a free appropriate public education. Under the Individuals with Disabilities Education Act (IDEA), an appropriate public education means specially designed instruction to meet the unique needs of the student with a disability. It also means educating the student with a disability in the least restrictive environment (LRE). That means educating the student with a disability, to the maximum extent appropriate, along side students without disabilities. Under the IDEA, educational services are planned by a team that includes the student's parents. That team discusses the student's educational needs, determines services to meet those needs, and writes those services into a plan called the Individualized Educational Program (IEP).

Two other laws, Section 504 of the Rehabilitation Act and the Americans with Disabilities Act (ADA), also require that students with disabilities receive a free appropriate public education, but those laws have a slightly different focus. They focus on ensuring that students with disabilities have equal access to educational services. Section 504 and the ADA are intended to ensure that students with disabilities receive educational services to meet their needs as adequately as the needs of children without disabilities are met. Section 504 and the ADA also require that students with disabilities receive services with students without disabilities. In addition, Section 504 and the ADA require that a plan is developed that outlines the services that will be provided to ensure the student with a disability has equal access to educational services.

There is no doubt that parents and educators want to do what is best for students with disabilities. But there can be disagreement over how to meet a student's needs and what is appropriate can be perceived differently depending on one's perspective. "Appropriate, like beauty, is in the eye of the beholder."[1] Throughout the process of serving students with disabilities, there are going to be disagreements. Most disagreements can be resolved without using formal complaints, due process hearings, litigation, and without lawyers. Unfortunately, there will also be times when educators are misinformed or make mistakes. Remember, "the best laid plans of mice and men…"

How to Use this Workbook

This workbook is for anyone who wants to avoid special education legal involvement. By knowing the legal requirements, parents and educators can work together for the benefit of students. This workbook is organized with a series of articles providing practical information about special education law. Then, actual cases are presented in a concise, story-telling format with the views of the players stated as arguments. The legal requirement is then listed. To understand the legal decisions, a brief description of the basics of special education law is provided. The reader can try to predict the outcome of the case based on what he or she has learned by reading the articles and the case scenarios. The answers are provided at the end of each case.

Conclusion: Litigation Prevention

It is neither cost, nor time effective for school personnel to be involved in legal problems. Following the prevention tips in this workbook helps school personnel to know what they can do to avoid conflicts. Using actual cases gives an accurate picture of what can happen from a legal perspective. When legal issues are resolved, teachers can teach and students can learn. Knowing what law applies is the first step to avoiding legal problems. When special education legal requirements are known and followed, everybody wins!

---

[1] Chapman, p. 42 *The Everyday Guide to Special Education Law*, Second Edition.

I

Avoiding Stormy IEP Meetings:

Tips for Chairing an IEP Meeting

Principal Fife was the captain of the good ship HMS Middle School. He knew his mission, keep the school ship shape, hatches battened down, and sailing straight. Through twenty years serving in her majesty's local education agency, he'd successfully weathered the storms sent his way. Why then had the IEP meeting he just chaired been such a disaster? He was assigned to act as the designee for the Director of Special Education and, though he had attended many IEP meetings, this was the first time he scheduled, planned, and chaired an IEP meeting for a student with a disability.

He thought he'd run a tight meeting. He invited only the essential professionals. To keep the meeting on time as well as non adversarial, he kept discussion to a minimum and discouraged the questioning of the professionals. After all, each professional was an expert in their area of service provision and their recommendations shouldn't be second guessed by others. Thanks to him the meeting was completed in ninety minutes (thirty minutes past the one hour he had announced at the outset as the time allotted for the meeting). So, what was the deal? Why did the parents leave angry and threatening to see a lawyer?

In the above scenario, Principal Fife wanted to have a productive Individualized Educational Program (IEP) meeting. He wanted to develop a good program for the student, but his emphasis on efficiency sacrificed quality and unnecessarily angered the student's parents. Sure, there are going to be disagreements in IEP meetings. Educational programming is not an exact science. You should expect that, at times, parents will disagree with the recommendations of the educational professionals and educational professionals will disagree with one another. But proactively seeking parent input in the IEP process can help you avoid unnecessary disagreements and help make those disagreements that may be necessary less disagreeable.

Eight Tips for Planning and Chairing an IEP Meeting

1. Schedule the meeting at a time reasonably convenient for the parents. The IDEA requires this and it makes good sense. Let the parents know in writing when the meeting is scheduled and make sure they know they can reschedule for another time and who to contact if they wish to reschedule. Then, if they ask, reschedule. You do not want parents to call the wrong person and be told the date is set, etched in stone, and cannot be changed.

2. Tell the parents, in writing, who the school district is inviting to the IEP meeting and what their role is. The parent may not know what role each professional plays in their child's life. You don't need to provide a biography of each IEP team member, but include their title and be sure the parents know they can find out more information if they wish.

3. Make sure all of the right people are invited to the IEP meeting. For example, if the student will be transitioning from elementary school to middle school next year, it might be wise for you to include some of the middle school teachers in this year's IEP. Or, if you expect a discussion regarding placing the student in a private or non-district program, make sure appropriate staff from that program attend the meeting to describe the program and answer questions. Parents and other professionals cannot make a decision about a placement in a vacuum.

4. Ask the parents if they would like other individuals to be invited to the meeting. The IDEA requires that "not less than one of the student's regular education teachers" attend the meeting, but students in middle school and high school often have more than one regular education teacher. The parent may want to have more than one regular education teacher. The IDEA also allows parents or school personnel to include on the IEP team other individuals who have knowledge or expertise about the child's special needs. For example, the child may be seeing a therapist privately and the parent may want that individual invited to the meeting. When it comes to IEP meetings more is not necessarily merrier, but too few is clearly not enough.

5. Do not set a time limit for the meeting. Try to schedule sufficient time, but if the IEP is not completed in that time, schedule another meeting to complete the IEP. Be sure that the parents and other professionals know that this IEP will not be rushed to completion.

6. Facilitate open discussion among all members of the IEP team. Encourage parents to ask questions of the professionals and the professionals to ask questions of the parents and each other.

7. Translate professional mumbo jumbo. Break down education speak so that all team members understand what is being said.

8. Remember whose child it is. Listen to the parents and treat them as you wish to be treated: as a professional. Parents are members of the team. Remember, that while school professionals want what's best for the child, they are not the parents. Professionals know the child as their student while at school and during the child's school career. But the parents will be the child's parents for life.

Using these tips will tell parents that you and the other educators in the IEP meeting really want what is best for their child and value the parents' input. If parents think that you are not open to their ideas, they can become frustrated and angry. Refusing to reschedule meetings or to invite individuals that the parents would like at the meeting sends a message that you don't really care. Since you do care, don't send that message. Also, listening to the parents, having the right people at the meeting, and facilitating open discussion will help ensure that a good plan is developed. There will be disagreements in IEP meetings. That's okay. There are times when IEP meetings may become rancorous and adversarial. That's okay too. But you don't want the meeting to become needlessly adversarial because you didn't seek parent input into putting the IEP team together and you didn't respectfully listen to the parents' concerns.

II

Discipline and Disability:

Determining When a Child's Misbehavior in School Is Related to His Disability

As a parent, Maria had a long rope but she was quickly nearing the end of it. The principal had just called and asked her to come to school and pick up her son, Jeremy, because the teacher said he was "out of control." Jeremy hadn't finished his work during class time and when the teacher told him he had to stay in during recess he threw his book at the chalkboard. Maria knew Jeremy could sometimes be a handful. He was in special education and had some emotional/behavioral issues, but this was the fourth time this fall that she'd been called, and Jeremy had now missed 10 days of school. This time the principal said he was suspended for another ten days and might be expelled or moved to a different school because his behavior was so disruptive.

While Maria knew that Jeremy's behavior was not acceptable, she believed it was related to his disability, and that there might be better ways to deal with it than withholding recess. Jeremy struggled to sit still through class and recess was a much-needed break. It didn't seem fair that he might be expelled for "misbehavior" that was not Jeremy's fault. Hadn't she heard that students with disabilities could not be punished for behavior that was a manifestation of their disability? Didn't the law require that, as a child with a disability, Jeremy was entitled to appropriate educational services?

The Individuals with Disabilities Education Act (IDEA) provides that all children with disabilities have a right to a free appropriate public education, including children who are suspended or expelled. The IDEA has specific procedures for school administrators to follow when disciplining children with disabilities. These procedures balance the need to keep schools safe with the right of children with disabilities to receive a free appropriate public education. There is a process to determine if a student's misconduct is a manifestation of the student's disability, and prevents children from being punished for "misbehavior" that is related to the child's disability. Unfortunately, the IDEA's procedures can be confusing. Here are some questions and answers regarding the manifestation determination process that should make the process clearer.

1. Why are there "special" rules for disciplining children with disabilities?

When Congress first enacted the Education for All Handicapped Children Act in 1975, it noted that children with disabilities were often suspended, expelled, or otherwise excluded from public education in our country merely because they had behavior problems. School officials had often unilaterally excluded children with disabilities from school without parent input or an opportunity to appeal. Congress wanted to ensure that all children with disabilities had access to a free appropriate public education. Moreover, Congress wanted to protect children with disabilities from the unilateral, speculative, and subjective decisions by school officials that had often caused them to be removed from school for behavior related to their disability.

2. Who makes the Manifestation Determination?

The manifestation determination is made by a group that includes the child's parent and the relevant members[2] of the child's Individualized Educational Program (IEP) team. The parent and school administrators decide which IEP team members will be included in the meeting.

---

[2] 34 CFR § 300.530(e)

3. *When must a Manifestation Determination be made?*

Whenever school officials make a disciplinary "change in placement,"[3] there must be a manifestation determination. A change in placement occurs whenever the school decides to remove or suspend a student with a disability from the student's educational placement for more than 10 school days. The 10 school days may be consecutive or over the course of a school year.

There must also be a manifestation determination if the student has been subjected to a series of removals that constitute a pattern. A pattern is determined if (a) the student is removed for more than 10 days in the school year; (b) the student's behavior is substantially similar to his behavior in previous incidents, and (c) considering the length of each removal, the total amount of time the student has been removed, and the proximity of the removals to one another, there appears to be a pattern of removing the student.

4. *How does the group decide if the student's misconduct is a manifestation of the student's disability?*

First, the group will review all of the relevant information in the student's file including any information included from the IEP, teacher observations, and information provided by the student's parents. Based on that review, the group will determine whether:[4]

• The student's misconduct was caused by or was directly or substantially related to the student's disability; or

• The misconduct was the direct result of the school district not implementing the student's IEP.

If the group determines that the misconduct was related to the student's disability or was the direct result of the IEP not being implemented, then the team will determine that the misconduct was a manifestation of the student's disability.

---

[3] 34 CFR § 300.530(e)
[4] 34 CFR § 300.530(e)

5. *If the student knows right from wrong and understands it is wrong to violate the student code of conduct, doesn't that mean his misconduct was not a manifestation of the disability?*

No, the student may know the behavior is wrong but the misconduct might still be directly related to his disability. For example, the student's disability may limit his ability to control the behavior. Or, perhaps IEP services, such as counseling, were never provided, causing the student's behavior to escalate beyond the student's control.

6. *What happens if the student's misconduct is determined to be a manifestation of the student's disability?* [5]

The student's IEP team will meet and unless there are special circumstances or the IEP team changes the student's educational placement, the student will return to the school program the student was in before the suspension. The IEP team will also conduct a Functional Behavioral Assessment and will implement a Behavior Intervention Plan for the student. A Functional Behavioral Assessment gathers information about the student's behavior to determine what function the student's behavior serves for the student. The Behavior Intervention Plan is the plan to provide support to the student to intervene with the behavior.

7. *What are special circumstances?* [6]

In disciplinary situations involving possession of weapons, illegal drugs, or when the student has caused a serious injury, the school may remove the student for up to 45 school days, even if the misconduct is a manifestation of the student's disability. The student must receive appropriate educational services after the first 10 school days that the student is removed.

---

[5] 34 CFR § 300.530(f)
[6] 34 CFR § 300.530(f)

8. *What if the group determines that the misconduct is NOT a manifestation of the student's disability?*

If the student's misconduct is not a manifestation of the student's disability, then the student may be disciplined the same as a student without a disability. But if expelled, the student is still entitled to receive a free appropriate public education. In many cases, the student's behavior is determined to be a manifestation of the student's disability. But, parents have the right to appeal[7] a decision that their child's behavior is not related to their child's disability. Hearings to resolve disagreements in the disciplinary process are expedited. That means the hearing must be held within 20 school days after it is requested, and the decision must be made within 10 school days after the hearing is completed.

Some school administrators pride themselves on a no-nonsense zero tolerance approach to discipline in their schools. In such an environment, normal childhood mischief can be mistaken for serious misconduct. For children with disabilities, disability related behavior can be confused with misconduct requiring discipline. Being aware and making sure your child's school is aware of the discipline procedures under the IDEA will help ensure your child's success in school.

---

[7] 34 CFR § 300.532

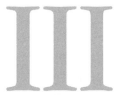

From the Outside Looking In:

Independent Educational Evaluations

The parents' right to obtain an Independent Educational Evaluation[8] (IEE) of their child is an important IDEA procedural safeguard.[9] School districts conduct evaluations[10] to provide information to the student's IEP team to determine whether a student has a disability and, if so, the services the student will need. Thus, a student's school program is largely based on the results of evaluations. An inaccurate or incomplete evaluation may lead to inappropriate services.

So, there are times when parents might be concerned that the school's evaluations do not accurately reflect their child's disability or educational needs. And, there are times when parents would just like a second opinion. An Independent Educational Evaluation[11] means an evaluation conducted by a qualified examiner who is not employed by the public agency responsible for educating the child. Thus, obtaining an Independent Educational Evaluation allows parents access to an evaluation conducted by someone outside of the school district and to provide that information to their child's IEP team.

Independent Educational Evaluations at Parent Expense

Parents have the right to obtain an Independent Educational Evaluation at their own expense and share it with the school district. If parents request an Independent Educational Evalu-

---

[8] 34 CFR § 300.502
[9] 34 CFR § 300.500 – 300.536
[10] 34 CFR § 300.300 – 300.328
[11] 34 CFR § 300.502

ation,[12] school districts are required to provide the parents with information about where they may obtain an independent evaluation. Moreover, if parents share their privately purchased evaluation with the school district, the IEP team must consider the results of the evaluation.[13] Considering the Independent Educational Evaluation, however, does not mean the IEP team must agree with it. If the IEP team disagrees with all or part of the Independent Educational Evaluation, the team should document why it did not accept the findings and recommendations of the Independent Educational Evaluation.

Additionally, if the parents share their privately purchased evaluation with the school district and there is a hearing regarding the child's program, the Independent Educational Evaluation may be presented by the parents or the school district as evidence at the hearing.[14]

Independent Educational Evaluations at Public Expense

If parents disagree with the evaluations done by the school district, the parents have the right to request an Independent Educational Evaluation to be paid at public expense.[15] If parents request an Independent Educational Evaluation at public expense, the school district must either (1) provide the Independent Educational Evaluation or (2) request a hearing to show that the school district's evaluation was appropriate.[16] Thus, if the district does not wish to pay the costs of the independent evaluation, the school district must request a hearing[17] to show that the district's evaluation is appropriate.

If parents obtain an evaluation at public expense, the district must consider the results of the evaluation in making educational decisions about the child. Again, the fact that the district must consider the evaluation does not mean that it must agree with its findings and recommendations. Finally, if there is a hearing regarding the child's program, the publicly funded Independent Educational Evaluation may be presented as evidence by the parents or the school district at the hearing.

---

[12] 34 CFR § 300.502
[13] 34 CFR § 300.502(c)(2)
[14] 34 CFR § 300.502(c)(2)
[15] 34 CFR § 300.502(a)(3)(ii)
[16] 34 CFR § 300.502(b)
[17] 34 CFR § 300.502(b)(2)(i)

What Does Public Expense Mean?

At public expense[18] means that the school district pays for the full cost of the Independent Educational Evaluation or ensures that the evaluation is provided at no cost to the parent. According to the Office of Special Education Programs (OSEP) in Letter to Heldman,[19] in a case in which an overnight trip was necessary to obtain the Independent Educational Evaluation, public expense may include covering the parents' related travel costs, including reasonable meal and lodging expenses. Parents are not entitled to unlimited evaluations at public expense. The IDEA 2004 clarified that parents are limited to only one Independent Educational Evaluation[20] each time the school district conducts an evaluation with which the parent disagrees.

May the Independent Evaluator Observe the Student in the Current Placement?

Under the IDEA regulations,[21] if the Independent Educational Evaluation is at public expense, "the criteria under which the evaluation is obtained, including the location of the evaluation and the qualifications of the examiner, must be the same as the criteria which the public agency uses when it initiates its evaluation." According to OSEP in Letter to Wessels,[22] this means if the school district (public agency) observed the student as part of its evaluation, or if the district's "assessment procedures make it permissible to have in-class observation of the child, the independent evaluator has the right to do so."

What if the district's procedures do not allow in-class observation? In that case, if the parent believes that in-class observation is necessary to assess the child, the parent can request a hearing to challenge the district's evaluation because it did not include in-class observation.

Conclusion

It has been my experience that sometimes school districts will purchase independent evaluations to obtain additional information on a child's educational

---

[18] 34 CFR § 300.502(a)(3)(ii)
[19] 20 IDELR 621(OSEP 1993)
[20] 34 CFR § 300.502(a)(1)
[21] 34 CFR § 300.502(e)
[22] 16 IDELR 735 (OSEP 1990)

needs. The IEP team wants to serve the child and may welcome an independent assessment to help design a program to meet the child's needs. Additionally, an independent evaluation can sometimes be useful to help resolve disagreements between a child's parents and the school. The opinion of an independent person, with "no ax to grind," may help the parents and the school resolve a disagreement and avoid the need to resort to lengthier dispute resolution procedures. An independent evaluation may be a very helpful tool for an IEP team to identify the needs of a student with a disability.

Case One:

Behavior Manifestation

Massachusetts State Educational Agency (2007)[23]

Due Process Hearing[24]

Facts of the Case

A male high school student, determined to have a Specific Learning Disability (SLD)[25] and Attention Deficit Hyperactivity Disorder (ADHD)[26] and with an outside psychologist's diag-

---

[23] Swansea Public Schools

[24] 47 IDELR 278

[25] According to IDEA Definitions of Disability Terms: Specific learning disability.

(i) General. Specific learning disability means a disorder in one or more of the basic psychological processes involved in understanding or in using language, spoken or written, that may manifest itself in an imperfect ability to listen, think, speak, read, write, spell, or to do mathematical calculations, including conditions such as perceptual disabilities, brain injury, minimal brain dysfunction, dyslexia, and developmental aphasia.

(ii) Disorders not included. Specific learning disability does not include learning problems that are primarily the result of visual, hearing, or motor disabilities; of mental retardation; of emotional disturbance; or of environmental, cultural, or economic disadvantage. 34 CFR 300.8(c)(10)

[26] According to IDEA Definitions of Disability Terms: Other health impairment means having limited strength, vitality, or alertness, including a heightened alertness to environmental stimuli, that results in limited alertness with respect to the educational environment, that—

    (i)   Is due to chronic or acute health problems such as asthma, attention deficit disorder or attention deficit hyperactivity disorder, diabetes, epilepsy, a heart condition, hemophilia, lead poisoning, leukemia, nephritis, rheumatic fever, sickle cell anemia, and Tourette syndrome; and

    (ii)   Adversely affects a child's educational performance. 34 CFR 300.8(c)(9)

nosis of Oppositional Defiant Disorder (ODD),[27] was eating pop-tarts in his "alternative program" class. The classroom was located in a large high school, but was separate from regular education classrooms. The special education teacher told the student to put the food away and the student responded angrily. The teacher told him to go to the back of the room to settle down. On his way to the back of the room, the student mumbled "I'm going to head butt you." The principal happened to be in the room, so he escorted the student to his office and suspended him for two days for threatening the teacher. On his way out of the building, the student went to his locker to get his belongings and called his mother on his cell phone to come pick him up. This occurred during passing period so there were many students in the hall. The student was talking loudly and using profanity as he spoke to his mother. The assistant principal, unaware of the suspension, heard the student and told him to hand over the cell phone and go to the office. The student threw the phone to the ground in anger. The assistant principal picked up the phone and the student repeated several times, "Give me my f-ing cell phone." The assistant principal backed away from the student who was reaching for his phone. She backed up against a wall and told the secretary to call the police. There was no physical contact or threat of any physical contact. The police arrived at the same time as the mother so the student went home with his mother. The student was suspended for 10 days for "threat of assault" of the assistant principal. His conduct was determined NOT to be a manifestation of his disability. He was then expelled for one year. The only question is whether the student's conduct was a manifestation of his disabilities.

---

[27] Definition from source used by psychologists, not special education teachers. Diagnostic and Statistical Manual of Mental Disorders, fourth Edition. Copyright 1994 American Psychiatric Association Diagnostic criteria for 313.81 Oppositional Defiant Disorder A. A pattern of negativistic, hostile, and defiant behavior lasting at least 6 months, during which four (or more) of the following are present:

(1) often loses temper
(2) often argues with adults
(3) often actively defies or refuses to comply with adults' requests or rules
(4) often deliberately annoys people
(5) often blames others for his or her mistakes or misbehavior
(6) is often touchy or easily annoyed by others
(7) is often angry and resentful
(8) is often spiteful or vindictive

Note: Consider a criterion met only if the behavior occurs more frequently than is typically observed in individuals of comparable age and developmental level. B. The disturbance in behavior causes clinically significant impairment in social, academic, or occupational functioning. C. The behaviors do not occur exclusively during the course of a Psychotic or Mood Disorder. D. Criteria are not met for Conduct Disorder, and, if the individual is age 18 years or older, criteria are not met for Antisocial Personality Disorder.

The school believes that the assistant principal was frightened and felt physically threatened. She was visibly shaken. The principal reported the incident as an abusive and violent attack. Even if the student's conduct was a manifestation of his disability, there is an exception for circumstances involving serious bodily injury. The special education teacher testified that violence and aggression are not associated with the labels Oppositional Defiant Disorder (ODD)/Attention Deficit Hyperactivity Disorder (ADHD), so there was no relationship between the student's conduct and the student's disability. The teacher testified as an expert on both categories (i.e., ODD/ADHD).

The mother stated that she could hear the assistant principal yelling at her son while her son was talking to her on the cell phone after he was suspended. She believes this further escalated her son and his behavior was a result of the assistant principal's aggression. The mother believes the 10-day suspension and the year-long expulsion deny her son a free appropriate public education (FAPE) which is a violation of IDEA.

Issue

Was the student's conduct a manifestation of his disability when a school administrator may have escalated the student's behavior?

Applicable Law Under IDEA

If a student is removed from school for more than 10 days, there must be a behavior manifestation meeting to determine if the student's conduct is a manifestation of his disability. If it is determined that "the conduct in question... had a direct and substantial relationship to...his disability," then his conduct is considered to be a manifestation of his disabilities.[28] If the conduct is a manifestation of his disabilities, he is returned to school. Exceptions include: 1) if parents and school agree to a different placement or 2) if drugs, weapons or serious bodily injury are involved.[29]

1. What is the outcome?

_____

_____

_____

_____

_____

---

[28] 8 34 CFR 300.530(e)(2)
[29] 20 USC 1415(k)(1)(G)(i)(ii)(iii)

2. *What should have been done to prevent legal involvement?*

_____

_____

_____

_____

_____

Outcome of Case One:

Behavior Manifestation

Outcome: The student's behavior was determined to be a manifestation of the disability. The administration's actions had the effect of further escalating the student's conduct. The student's threatening behavior must be viewed within the context of the preceding events. The assistant principal's confrontation of the student while he was in a highly agitated, even hysterical, condition caused the student to lose all ability to self-regulate. Student's special education teacher was not persuasive due to her limited knowledge of Oppositional Defiant Disorder (ODD) which is not a special education category.

- Student should have been allowed to leave the building after being suspended;

- Student should have been allowed to eat his pop-tarts; and

- Special education teacher should not have testified about Oppositional Defiant Disorder since it is not a special education category.

V

Case Two:

Exclusion

Massachusetts State Educational Agency (2008)[30]

Facts of the Case

A student determined to have an Emotional Disturbance (ED) was suspended following an altercation with a teacher on June 13th, the last day of school. A behavior manifestation determination meeting was held and it was decided that the student's conduct WAS a manifestation of his disability. School was concluded for the year. The principal did not allow the student to return to school in September. The principal decided on his own to give the student 10 hours per week of homebound services. No meeting was held with parents or other school staff. The parents filed a complaint in November wanting monetary damages because their son was improperly excluded from school. The parents also wanted compensatory educational services. The school states, "We are providing homebound services so the student is receiving a Free Appropriate Public Education." Parents want a tort (personal injury money) settlement for improper exclusion from school.

---

[30] Milton Public Schools 49 IDELR 236

Issue

Can parents receive monetary damages because their child was excluded from school due to a procedural violation of IDEA?

Applicable Law Under IDEA

"After a manifestation determination, the IEP team shall return the child to the placement from which the child was removed, unless the parent and the Local Education Agency (LEA) agree to a change of placement as part of the modification of the Behavior Intervention Plan (BIP)." Exceptions include special circumstances involving a weapon at school, drugs, or serious bodily injury.[31] A change of placement, such as homebound services, requires an Individualized Educational Program (IEP) meeting.[32] The school cannot exclude a student from school without following IDEA procedures.[33] Parents cannot get tort money[34] under IDEA.

1. What is the outcome?

_____

_____

_____

_____

---

[31] 20 USC 1415(k)(1)(F)
[32] 20 USC 1415(k)(1)
[33] Bd. Of Educ. V. Rowley, 458 U.S. 176, 206 (1982)
[34] Money for personal injury

2. *What should have been done to prevent legal involvement?*

_____

_____

_____

_____

Outcome of Case Two:

Exclusion

Outcome: No money was awarded. Compensatory services are to be arranged between the school and the family. The student was denied Free Appropriate Public Education (FAPE) because there was a change in placement without an Individualized Educational Program (IEP) meeting. This was an IDEA procedural violation.

- The principal should have allowed the student back in school after being suspended;

- The principal should have followed IDEA procedures; and

- The principal should have known homebound services are considered a change of placement so he had to have an IEP meeting.

VI

Case Three:

Behavior Intervention Plans

Kingsport City School System v. J.R.,[35] *(2008)*

Facts of the Case

A high school male, receiving special education services, has a Behavior Intervention Plan (BIP)[36] to improve his social skills. The Behavior Intervention Plan indicates the student will refrain from name-calling, the student will refrain from contact with peers, and the student will report threats to staff. The student begins ninth grade and in the first week of school calls a peer a "faggot" resulting in the student being assaulted by the peer. Following this assault, the student has a fight in the cafeteria with his girlfriend and indicates he is going to "kill the f-ing bitch." The student is suspended for this threat. When he returns to school, the female friends of his (now) ex-girlfriend assault him. The girls are suspended. Next, the brother of one of the girls who was suspended assaults the student. At this point, the student is moved into a special

---

[35] 51 IDELR 77 (Eastern Dist. TN, 2008)

[36] Definition: A *Behavior Intervention Plan (BIP)* takes the observations made in a <u>Functional Behavioral Assessment</u> and turns them into a concrete plan of action for managing a student's behavior. A BIP may include ways to change the environment to keep behavior from starting in the first place, provide positive reinforcement to promote good behavior, employ planned ignoring to avoid reinforcing bad behavior, and provide supports needed so that the student will not be driven to act out due to frustration or fatigue. When a behavior plan is agreed to, the school and staff are legally obligated to follow it, and consequences of not following it should not be inflicted on the student. www.specialchildren.about.com

program at the high school. On his first day, he goes to the bus stop where he is again assaulted. The parents requested and received homebound services for two hours daily. The parents requested a Due Process Hearing for not complying with the Individualized Educational Program (IEP) because the school's "hostile, dangerous and harassing environment" prevented their son from attending school which denied their son a Free Appropriate Public Education (FAPE). At the beginning of tenth grade, the boy prepared to return to school. A new Behavior Intervention Plan was created that assigned a full-time shadow to the student. The shadow would follow the student to all classes, the bathroom and the cafeteria. The parents claimed the new Behavior Intervention Plan was also a violation of IDEA and denied their son a Free Appropriate Public Education. The issue is whether the Behavior Intervention Plan provided a Free Appropriate Public Education.

The school states, "We are providing a shadow for the student so he will be safe. We also put in the Behavior Intervention Plan that he needs to stop calling other students names. This will keep him safe. He is not allowed to have contact with many of his peers which also keeps him safe. If another student threatens him, he has to tell us and we will take care of it." The school psychologist testified that the shadow is inappropriate, counseling is needed, and threat reporting is a burden.

The parents stated they were being threatened with truancy proceedings if they didn't agree to the Behavior Intervention Plan (BIP) with the shadow. Parents stated that their son cannot receive a Free Appropriate Public Education while being followed by a shadow. Parents want a better Behavior Intervention Plan.

Issue

> *Does this new Behavior Intervention Plan (BIP) provide educational benefit?*

Applicable Law Under IDEA

The IEP team shall "in the case of a child whose behavior impedes the child's learning or that of others, consider the use of positive behavioral interventions and supports, and other strategies, to address that behavior."[37]

---

[37] 20 USC 1414(d)(3)(B)(i)

If the school, the parent, and the IEP Team make a determination that conduct was a manifestation of a child's disability, the IEP Team must either conduct a Functional Behavioral Assessment (FBA), and implement a Behavior Intervention Plan (BIP) for the child; or if a Functional Behavioral Assessment and Behavior Intervention Plan were already developed, review the Behavior Intervention Plan, and modify it, as necessary, to address the behavior.[38]

According to Rowley,[39] the school must provide an Individualized Educational Program (IEP) that is "reasonably calculated to provide educational benefit." Courts cannot substitute their own notions of sound educational policy for those of school authorities. The court must rely on what the school authorities state regarding effective educational policies.

1. *What is the outcome?*

_____

_____

_____

_____

2. *What should have been done to prevent legal involvement?*

_____

_____

_____

_____

[38] 34 CFR §300.530(f)(1)
[39] *Bd. Of Educ. V. Rowley*, 458 U.S. 176 (1982).

Outcome of Case Three:

Behavior Intervention Plans

Outcome: The Behavior Intervention Plan (BIP) violated the Individuals with Disabilities Education Act (IDEA) because it denied the student a Free Appropriate Public Education (FAPE) so the Behavior Intervention Plan must be modified. The Behavior Intervention Plan, for this student, is for the purpose of improving social skills, so social skills training must be provided, not social isolation (i.e., no contact with peers). The shadow prohibits the goal of social interaction, according to the school's own psychologist, so eliminate the shadow. A new Behavior Intervention Plan must be written.

- If the current Behavior Intervention Plan is not effective, review and revise as necessary. If a Behavior Intervention Plan goal is to improve peer interaction, then counseling and social skills training should have been provided, not social isolation;

- The staff should have considered that a shadow (e.g., paraprofessional) may prohibit a student's opportunity to learn to socialize; and

- The burden for reporting threats should not be on the student so it should not have been on the Behavior Intervention Plan.

Case Four:

Behavior Intervention Plans

M.C. v. Central Regional School District, (1996)[40]

Facts of the Case

A student was identified as having Attention Deficit Hyperactivity Disorder (ADHD) in second grade and began receiving special education services. In fourth grade she was also determined as having a learning disability. The Individualized Educational Program (IEP) from eighth to tenth grade contained behavioral strategies that were the same every year. The school psychologist wrote in her report that the student's behaviors were the same as the previous year (e.g., not handing in homework, losing assignments). Her progress clearly decreased in ninth and tenth grade. Her tenth grade IEP indicated "Student needs to become more responsible, Student needs to apply strategies, Student needs to concentrate." An IEP was developed for her eleventh grade year before school started. It was never implemented because the student attended private school for eleventh grade.

The parents claim that their daughter did not receive a Free Appropriate Public Education because, even though she regressed over several years, the school district never modified her Individualized Educational Program. Parents want tuition reimbursement for eleventh grade and compensatory services for ninth and tenth grade.

---

[40] *M.C. v. Cent. Reg'l Sch. Dist.*, 81 F.3d 89 (3rd Cir. 1996).

School personnel states: "You can lead a horse to water, but you can't make him drink." School personnel claims they did not act in bad faith because this case involved the most intervention the special education teacher ever had for a student. School claims they did everything they could but the student took no responsibility.

Issue

Are parents entitled to private school reimbursement when IEP's do not indicate educational progress?

Applicable Law Under IDEA

"The IEP team must review the child's IEP periodically, but not less than annually, to determine whether the annual goals for the child are being achieved and to revise the IEP, as appropriate, to address any lack of expected progress toward the annual goals and in the regular education curriculum."[41]

"An IEP must include a statement of measurable annual goals, including academic and functional goals designed to meet the child's needs that result from the child's disability to enable the child to be involved in and make progress in the regular education curriculum and meet each of the child's other educational needs that result from the child's disability."[42]

"An IEP must also include a description of how the child's progress toward meeting the annual goals will be measured."[43]

The Behavior Intervention Plan (BIP) must include positive interventions and be used consistently by all teachers. In this circuit, it had been held that "the right to compensatory education accrues when the school knows or should have known that its IEP is not providing an appropriate education."[44] Parental agreement to the IEP does not mean there is no IDEA violation. The district is responsible for the IEP because parents may not be sufficiently sophisticated to understand the process.

---

[41] 34 CFR § 300.324(b)
[42] 34 CFR § 300.320(2)
[43] 34 CFR § 300.320(3)
[44] *M.C. v. Cent. Reg'l Sch. Dist.*, 81 F.3d 89 (3rd Cir. 1996).

1. *What is the outcome?*

_____

_____

_____

_____

2. *What should have been done to prevent legal involvement?*

_____

_____

_____

_____

Outcome of Case Four:

Behavior Intervention Plans

Outcome: The judge stated that "this IEP requires the student to quench her thirst at an empty well." The district blamed the student for acting like a child with a disability. The Behavior Intervention Plan must shape desired behaviors and use positive rather than negative consequences. The district should have known the program was not effective. The court granted tuition reimbursement and compensatory services.

- The school should have developed a Functional Behavioral Assessment (FBA) and a Behavior Intervention Plan (BIP) because the student's behavior was impacting learning (the disability category doesn't matter);

- The District should have known the program it was providing was not effective; and

- Parent involvement and approval did not mean the IEP was appropriate so the district should not have assumed so.

VIII

House Passes HR 4247
Keeping All Students Safe Act

On March 7, 2010 the House of Representatives voted 262 to 153 to pass HR 4247, the Keeping All Students Safe Act.[45] This legislation was introduced in December 2009 as the Preventing Harmful Restraint and Seclusion in Schools Act.[46] The legislation directs the Secretary of Education to establish minimum standards that:

1. prohibit elementary and secondary school personnel from managing students by using mechanical or chemical restraint, physical restraint or escort that restricts breathing, or aversive behavioral intervention that compromises student health and safety;

2. prohibits school staff from using physical restraint unless needed to eliminate an imminent danger of physical injury to the student or others;

3. requires states to ensure school staff receive training in crisis intervention and effective student management techniques;

---

[45] Keeping All Students Safe Act of 2010, H.R. 4247, 111th Cong. (2010).
[46] Preventing Harmful Restraint and Seclusion in Schools Act of 2009, H.R. 4247, 111th Cong. (2009).

4. prohibits physical restraint and seclusion from being written into a student's IEP as a planned intervention;

5. requires schools to establish procedures to notify parents if physical restraint or seclusion is imposed on their child;

6. requires states, within two years, to establish procedures to monitor and enforce these standards regulating the use of restraint and seclusion; and

7. gives Protection and Advocacy Systems the authority under the Developmental Disabilities Assistance and Bill of Rights Act of 2000 to investigate, monitor, and enforce the Act's protections of students.

Prior to the introduction of the Act, the Secretary of Education requested that State Education Agencies review their restraint and seclusion policies and report to the Department of Education. Based on the response to that request, it is clear that states do not have uniform and effective policies regulating the use of abusive restraint in schools. For a summary of current state policies on the use of restraint, see Summary Table of Seclusion and Restraint Statutes, Regulations, Policies and Guidance, by State and Territories.[47] The Act will need to be approved by the Senate, where Senator Chris Dodd has introduced a Senate version of the Keeping All Students Safe Act.

NOTE: Senator Dodd withdrew this legislation in November 2010, and no further action was taken before adjournment of the 111th Congress.

---

[47] U.S. Department of Education, http://www2.ed.gov/policy/seclusion/seclusion-state-summary.html

Case Five:

The Restraint Case

Maryland State Educational Agency (2006)[48]

State Complaints Officer Investigation

Facts of the Case

A boy in first grade is determined to have Attention Deficit Hyperactivity Disorder (ADHD) and exhibits ADHD characteristics including not sitting still, running around, not following directions, and not paying attention. The boy had a Behavior Intervention Plan (BIP) which is part of an Individualized Educational Program (IEP). His mother participated in review and revise meetings for her son's IEP/BIP with the school in November, January, and March. The boy showed measurable progress. The boy then began second grade with a new teacher. Prior to September 22, the boy was physically restrained fourteen times and dismissed from school early three times. Most of the restraints involved the teacher putting the child in a "basket hold" when the student wouldn't sit where the teacher directed him to sit. The documentation shows that the teacher would hold the boy until he verbally complied. The physical restraints were conducted by staff trained in restraint techniques. Documentation showed the boy was restrained for running around, disrespectful behavior and not following directions. The staff was unaware of district and

---

[48] Cecil County Public Schools 5 ECLPR 37

state procedures for the use of restraint. The behaviors prompting restraint were not consistent with the circumstances in which restraint can be used in the state. There was no documentation of less intrusive procedures as required by law in the state in which the incident occurred. The mother requested a Behavior Intervention Plan review on September 22nd and the school scheduled it for November 3rd. The mother filed an expedited Due Process complaint because the school did not review the IEP/BIP prior to the fourteen restraints and refused to meet with her until November because they were "too busy." She also complained that state regulations for restraint were not followed.

The school stated that the restraints were justified and documented by staff trained in using restraints. Early dismissals were not documented because when a student leaves school early due to a discipline issue, it does not require documentation. The mother's request for a meeting was honored but everyone was busy so it couldn't be scheduled until November 3rd.

Parent wanted the Behavior Intervention Plan (BIP) to be reviewed and revised because the boy was not experiencing educational benefit. Additionally, parents stated staff did not follow state and district policies for using restraint. Also, early dismissals should have been documented because they were related to discipline. The boy was not suspended, but was being sent home early which denied him educational services.

Issues

> *Were state restraint guidelines followed? Since there was no progress over time, should the Behavior Intervention Plan have been revised?*

Applicable Law Under IDEA

"The public agency must ensure that an Individualized Educational Program (IEP) team reviews and revises, as appropriate, a student's IEP to address any lack of expected progress toward achieving the annual goals, the results of any re-evaluation, information about the student provided to or by the parents, or the student's anticipated needs."[49]

The Individuals with Disabilities Education Act (IDEA) does not regulate restraint and seclusion; state education laws control the use of physical restraints.

---

[49] 20 USC § 1414(d) and 34 CFR §300.343

1. *What is the outcome?*

    _____

    _____

    _____

    _____

2. *What should have been done to prevent legal involvement?*

    _____

    _____

    _____

    _____

Outcome of Case Five:

The Restraint Case

Outcome: School must review the Individualized Educational Program (IEP)/ Behavior Intervention Plan (BIP) within 30 days in this case and not wait until the scheduled meeting in November. A Corrective Action Plan for the district must be established to make sure restraint and seclusion policies are aligned with state regulations, disseminated to staff, implemented, and evaluated.

- School staff should have known their state regulations for restraint and seclusion before actually using restraints;

- The special education teacher should have reviewed and revised the Behavior Intervention Plan (BIP) as needed. Clearly, this should have occurred prior to the 14 restraints. The IEP team should have met to review the Behavior Intervention Plan as the mother requested before November; and

- The staff should have used positive strategies with the boy and only have used restraint when it complied with state regulations.

X

Getting the Most Out of the Least Restrictive Environment

Brenda tossed her parent folder on to the kitchen table and then slid into the sofa, pleased but exhausted. She had just returned from "Back to School Night" at her sons' middle school. This was the first year that Jeremy, her 11-year-old, was attending his neighborhood school. Jeremy had autism and had not attended elementary school with his older brother, Sam, but this year both her boys would go to the same school.

"Back to School Night" was the night before the first day of school and gave parents and kids an opportunity to visit each class and to meet the new teachers. Brenda had already met most of Jeremy's new middle school teachers because the teachers had attended his Individualized Educational Program (IEP) meeting last spring to help plan for his move to middle school.

In fact, the middle school regular education teachers had played a key role in including Jeremy in their classes at the middle school. Brenda had always wanted Jeremy and Sam to attend the same school. She knew that the Individuals with Disabilities Education Act (IDEA) required that children with disabilities go to school with children without disabilities and attend their neighborhood school, if possible. She liked the program provided at the elementary school where the school district had centralized services for elementary aged students with autism. Though it required some support services, Brenda had successfully pushed for Jeremy to be included in regular education classes and activities with students without disabilities at the elementary school.

But, she didn't like that the program wasn't in their neighborhood school. Brenda had planned that at Jeremy's IEP meeting last spring she would push for him to go to the neighborhood middle school with Sam. To Brenda's pleasant surprise, the middle school principal had encouraged the middle school teachers to attend Jeremy's spring IEP meeting. So, at "Back to School Night" Brenda and Jeremy already knew most of his new teachers. Brenda, still on the sofa, crossed her fingers and thought "So far, so good."

Many families struggle to make sure their children who have disabilities go to school along side of children without disabilities. The following are seven tips for using the IEP process to get the most out of the least restrictive environment.

1. Make sure the IEP team follows the appropriate process in determining the least restrictive environment for your child. The IEP team arrives at the least restrictive environment, step by step. Legally, the term "least restrictive environment" means that to the maximum extent appropriate, children with disabilities are educated with children without disabilities. It also means that before deciding to remove a child with a disability from regular education and placing the child in a special class or educating him separately, the IEP team must consider using supplementary aids and services. Thus, determining the least restrictive environment for a child with a disability is a process. The IEP team starts from the premise that the student will attend a regular classroom. If there is a question whether the student's education can be achieved satisfactorily in the regular education classroom, then the first step the IEP team takes is to consider providing supplementary aids and services to support the student and teachers in the regular classroom.

2. Make sure the IEP team considers providing supplementary aids and services[50] before removing your child from the regular classroom. Supplementary aids and services include teacher training and support, itinerant instruction, modified curriculum, paraprofessional support, and assistive technology. These are supports

---

[50] 34 CFR § 300.42

that are provided in regular classrooms and other education-related settings, including extracurricular and nonacademic activities, to enable children with disabilities to learn successfully with children without disabilities. These supports can be provided to help the regular education teacher as well as the child.

3. Make sure a regular education teacher is a member of the IEP team. The IDEA (Individuals with Disabilities Education Act) requires that not less than one of the child's regular education teachers be a member of the IEP team if the child is or may be participating in regular education.[51] The regular education teacher is a key team member for two reasons. First, the regular education teacher should understand why the child needs certain services, accommodations, aids, and supports. For example, if the regular education teacher understands why a student needs to have a modified curriculum or needs a note taker, the teacher is more likely to make sure the service or accommodation is provided. Second, the regular education teacher needs to listen and contribute to discussions determining supplementary aids and services, program modifications and other support for school staff. Moreover the regular education teacher should be involved in discussing behavioral interventions and supports for the child. It would be difficult for the IEP team to determine what support a regular teacher needed without that teacher's input.

4. If necessary, include more than one regular education teacher on the IEP team. Middle school and high school students often have more than one teacher. The IDEA requires that not less than one of the child's regular education teachers be included on the team but, in some circumstances, it may be important that more than one regular education teacher participate in the meeting. For example, if your child has a behavior intervention plan, it is important that all of your child's teachers are aware of that plan and how to implement it.

---

[51] 34 CFR § 300.321(a)(2), 300.324(a)(3)

5. Make sure that the IEP team discusses including your child in nonacademic and extracurricular activities with children without disabilities. These activities include meals, recess, counseling services, athletics, transportation, health services, recreational activities, and special interest groups and clubs that are school-sponsored. As it does for academic services, the IDEA requires that supplementary aids or services be provided to support your child's participation in nonacademic and extracurricular activities with children without disabilities.[52]

6. Don't forget field trips, assemblies and other similar activities! Sometimes children with disabilities are left out of field trips and assemblies because some school staff, inexperienced in working with children with disabilities, are concerned with the student's behavior. If this is a concern, the IEP team should discuss how supplementary aids and services can support the student and teacher so that the child can participate in the field trip or assembly with students without disabilities. Again, if the child's regular education teachers are members of the IEP team, they can participate in discussing the supports they or the student may need to successfully participate in these activities.

7. Make sure that the IEP team adequately considers placing your child in the neighborhood school. The IDEA requires that children with disabilities attend the school they would attend if they did not have a disability.[53] This is true unless the IEP requires some other arrangement. So, the IEP team should place a child in the neighborhood school unless the team determines that some another arrangement is educationally required. If another arrangement is needed, then the IDEA requires that the child attend school as close as possible to the child's home.

Finally, remember that determining the least restrictive environment for a child is a team process reached step-by-step. Start with the assumption that the child will go to the neighborhood school and be in the regular classroom. If supports are needed to make that setting successful, then the team discusses those supports, proceeding one step at a time.

---

[52] 34 CFR § 300.117
[53] 34 CFR § 300.116

Case Six:

Least Restrictive Environment

Murray v. Montrose County School District,[54] *(1995)*

Facts of the Case

A boy with multiple disabilities (defined as physical disabilities and cognitive disabilities) attends his neighborhood school until second grade when the school district determined the student should attend a school 10 miles away because there was a program for students with severe needs located there that was determined to be more appropriate for the student. The Individualized Education Program (IEP) team voted (5-4) for the student to attend the school away from his neighborhood. The neighborhood school claimed they could not meet the student's needs for an appropriate program or accessibility. The parents wanted their son to remain at the neighborhood school with his friends and siblings. Parents filed a complaint for violating the Individuals with Disabilities Act (IDEA) and the Least Restrictive Environment (LRE) provision. The case went through several judicial levels while the student continued to attend his neighborhood school.[55] In November of third grade, the IEP team determined that the IEP could now be implemented at the neighborhood school.

---

[54] 51 F.3d 921 (10th Cir. 1995)
[55] Due Process, Administrative Law Judge, Federal District Court

Parents claimed the Least Restrictive Environment (LRE) mandate presumes the LRE is located in the neighborhood school. Parents agreed with the IEP and the time allocated for regular education and special education services, but did not want the transfer. School personnel claimed the LRE statute says nothing about neighborhood schools so there is no legal requirement for a student to remain at a neighborhood school.

Issue

> *Do students with disabilities have the right to attend their neighborhood school when the magnet program for students with disabilities is located at another school?*

Applicable Law Under IDEA

"To the maximum extent appropriate, children with disabilities…are educated with children who are not disabled, and that special classes, separate schooling or other removal of children with disabilities from the regular educational environment occurs only when the nature or severity of the disability is such that education in regular classes with the use of supplementary aids and services cannot be achieved satisfactorily."[56]

---

[56] 20 USC 1412(5)(B)

1. *What is the outcome?*

    _____

    _____

    _____

    _____

2. *What should have been done to prevent legal involvement?*

    _____

    _____

    _____

    _____

Outcome of Case Six:

Least Restrictive Environment

Outcome: The case was dismissed a year after the complaint was filed because the IEP team determined that the IEP could be implemented at the neighborhood school.

- The team was only one vote short of keeping the student at the neighborhood school so maybe a teacher should have provided that vote in the first place;

- The school should have considered ways to meet the student's needs at the neighborhood school; and

- The school should have deferred to the parent since the parents got what they wanted a year later. By fighting with the parents, time and money were wasted for legal proceedings when the school agreed with the original parent request in the end.

Looking at the Trees in the Forest Grove Decision

In 2009 the Supreme Court ruled in *Forest Grove v T.A.*,[57] that the IDEA authorizes reimbursement of private school tuition to parents when: (1) the public school fails to provide appropriate special education services to the child; and (2) the private school program placement is appropriate. Importantly, this is true regardless of whether the child previously received special education or related services from the public school. Thus, parents should not be faced with the choice of placing their child in an inappropriate program, before seeking appropriate services from a private school.

This decision, however, does not mean that parents may ignore the public school program, place their child in a private program without notice to the school district, and just send the district the bill for the private school tuition. The decision clarifies that in order to qualify for private school tuition reimbursement, parents must (1) establish that, before the student was placed in the private program, the school district did not make an appropriate public education available to the student and (2) the program provided by the private school is appropriate.[58]

For example, in the facts underlying the *Forest Grove*[59] decision, the student had difficulties in school from the time he was in kindergarten through his junior year of high school. His teachers often commented he had difficulty paying attention in class and completing his assign-

---

[57] *Forest Grove School District v. T.A.*, 129 S. Ct. 2484 (2009).

[58] 34 CFR § 300.148(b)

[59] *Forest Grove School District v. T.A.*, 129 S. Ct. 2484 (2009).

ments. Because his difficulties in school worsened when he entered high school, he was evaluated by a school psychologist at the end of his freshman year. The psychologist reviewed his school records and administered several cognitive ability tests, but decided the student did not need further testing for learning disabilities or attention deficit hyperactive disorder (ADHD). Thus, the student was found to be ineligible for special education. While the family did not appeal the decision at that time, it was later found by the hearing officer that the school district evaluation was legally inadequate because it did not address all areas of suspected disability, including ADHD.

The student completed his sophomore school year but his problems worsened during his junior year. The family sought private professional advice resulting in the student being diagnosed with ADHD and other disabilities related to learning and memory. Since the private therapist recommended a structured residential learning environment, the parents enrolled their son in a private academy for children with special needs. Then, four days after enrolling their son in the private academy, the parents gave *written notice* to the school district of the private placement. The parents later requested a due process hearing regarding their son's eligibility for special education services.

While awaiting the hearing, the school district re-evaluated the student and again found him ineligible for special education services and did not develop an IEP. Since the district did not offer special education services, the parents continued his placement in the private academy. At the conclusion of the hearing and after considering the testimony of numerous experts, the hearing officer issued a decision that the student was eligible for special education services because his ADHD adversely affected his educational performance.

Thus, the hearing officer concluded the school district had violated the IDEA by finding the student ineligible for special education services and by not providing those services. Since the school district did not provide the student with a free appropriate public education and the private placement was appropriate, the hearing officer ordered the school district to reimburse the parents the cost of the private school tuition.

To reach that result (to establish that the school had failed to offer an appropriate program and the private placement was appropriate), the parents bore the cost of a private evaluation, the cost of placement in a private school, the cost of an attorney and the experts who testified at the hearing, and the emotional wear and tear of the judicial process.

Financial and emotional cost continues because the case was remanded to the district court in order to decide the amount of tuition reimbursement. The IDEA provides[60] a number of factors that may result in the cost of tuition reimbursement being reduced or denied. Before removing their child from the public school, parents need to give adequate notice to the school district that the parents are rejecting the school district's placement and they intend to place their child in a private program at public expense. Parents may provide that notice at an IEP meeting[61] or, as in the *Forest Grove* scenario, in writing.[62]

Another factor in determining the amount of tuition reimbursement is if, before the child is removed from the public school program, the school district asked to evaluate the student and the parents refused.[63]

The Supreme Court remanded the case to the district court to consider these factors in determining the amount of tuition to be reimbursed to this family.

In conclusion, I believe this is a wonderful decision for the educational rights of children with disabilities. If a public program is inadequate, parents should not be faced with the choice of placing their child in that program before seeking placement in a private program. But, as the family in *Forest Grove* found, it is likely to be an uphill battle to establish both the inadequacy of the public school program and the appropriateness of the private placement.

---

[60] 34 CFR § 300.148(d)
[61] 34 CFR § 300.148(d)(1)(i)
[62] 34 CFR § 300.148(d)(1)(ii)
[63] 34 CFR § 300.148(d)(2)

Special Education Services in the Summer:

The IDEA and Extended School Year

Summer is rapidly approaching. For most children, summer means time off from school. But for some students with disabilities, interrupting their school program during the summer break jeopardizes the benefit they receive from that program during the regular school year. These students need services during the summer to receive a Free Appropriate Public Education. Services provided in the summer are called Extended School Year services or ESY services. Extended School Year services are special education and related services that are provided to a child with a disability beyond the normal school year of the school district.

The first court cases[64] addressing Extended School Year services involved students with disabilities who, during the summer, lost skills they had learned during the previous school year. As a result of this loss of skills during the summer, the students were unable to benefit from their school program. These cases established a regression/recoupment standard for establishing the need for ESY. The student lost skills during the summer, or regressed, so significantly that the student could not reasonably make up, or recoup, that loss the following school year.

The courts noted that all students regress some during extended absences from school. Most students can make up that loss, in a reasonable amount of time, when they return to school. If it takes a student with a disability significantly longer to make up the loss, that student may

---

[64] *Battle v. Pennsylvania*, 629 F.2d 269 (3rd Cir. 1980) *cert. denied*, 452 U.S. 968 (1981), *Alamo Heights Independent School District v. State Board of Education*, 790 F.2d 1153 (5th Cir. 1986).

be entitled to Extended School Year services. Thus, students who regressed that significantly were entitled to services during the summer as part of receiving a Free Appropriate Public Education.

Later court decisions[65] allowed students to receive Extended School Year services without first being out of school during the summer months. If the IEP team could predict that the student was likely to regress, Extended School Year services could be included on the IEP. Planning teams could look at how the student performed after being out of school during holidays, or illnesses. Based on how the student performed upon returning to school, the IEP team could predict whether the student would be eligible for Extended School Year services.

More recent court cases include factors, other than just regression/recoupment, in determining Extended School Year eligibility. The Tenth Circuit Court of Appeals, in *Johnson v. Independent School District No. 4*,[66] included factors such as:

- the degree of the student's impairment and the ability of the student's parents to provide educational structure at home;

- the student's rate of progress, the student's behavioral and physical problems;

- the availability of alternative resources;

- the ability of the student to interact with students without disabilities;

- the areas of the student's curriculum which need continuous attention; and

- the student's vocational needs.

The Court in *Johnson*[67] also looked at whether the service being requested for the Extended School Year was extraordinary to this particular student or was an integral part of a program for students with this disability. If the service was an integral part of the program for students with this disability, it could be required to be provided during the summer.

---

[65] *Polk, v. Central Susquehanna Intermediate Unit 16*, 853 F.2d 171 (3rd Cir. 1988).

[66] *Johnson v. Independent School District No. 4*, 921 F.2d 1022 (10th Cir. 1990), *cert. denied* 111 S.Ct. 1685 (1991).

[67] *Johnson v. Independent School District No. 4*, 921 F.2d 1022 (10th Cir. 1990), *cert. denied* 111 S.Ct. 1685 (1991).

Under the IDEA 2004, Extended School Year services[68] must be provided only if a student's IEP team determines, on an individual basis, that Extended School Year services are needed for the student to receive an appropriate education. The school district may not: (1) limit Extended School Year services to students with particular categories of disability; or (2) unilaterally limit the type, amount, or duration of the Extended School Year services. Additionally, since Extended School Year services are part of providing a free appropriate public education, the services must be provided according to an IEP and at no cost to the student's parents.

Extended School Year services are not intended to continue the progress the student made during the normal school year through the summer. Rather, Extended School Year services are required to prevent jeopardizing progress the student has already made during the normal school year. Parents who believe their child may need Extended School Year services should make sure this topic is discussed at the IEP meeting. If the student has not already been out of school for a summer, parents should make sure the student's teachers are tracking the student's performance after school holidays and absences. This information is necessary to predict future regression.

---

[68] 34 CFR § 300.106

XIV

AT Is Where It's At: Obtaining Assistive Technology for Students with Disabilities

Sometimes things worked out like they were supposed to and Sara was pleased. She had expected to have a fight on her hands as she went into Gracie's Individualized Educational Program (IEP) meeting. Gracie was six and because of multiple disabilities, she wasn't able to talk. But just because Gracie didn't talk didn't mean she couldn't communicate. Gracie communicated by using a picture board developed by a speech therapist who worked with Gracie when she was three and in preschool. The picture board had worked fairly well, but Gracie was now finishing first grade. Gracie's skills had grown and the tasks she needed to perform had become more complex as she advanced in school. Sara wanted the school to look into providing a more sophisticated communication system for Gracie as she entered second grade. Sara was concerned the school staff would be reluctant to explore what might be a more costly communication system.

But to Sara's surprise, the IEP team shared her concerns and recommended a complete evaluation of Gracie's assistive technology (AT) needs, including assessing her communication system. The assistive technology assessment was to be completed before the end of this school year and the team would meet again to review the results of the evaluation and plan services accordingly. As always, Sara still worried that things might not turn out as she hoped, but she knew that getting a good evaluation was the first step in getting appropriate services for Gracie. For right now, she was confident the school was doing its best for Gracie.

The IDEA and Assistive Technology

Under the Individuals with Disabilities Education Act (IDEA), schools are required to provide assistive technology services for children with disabilities. Assistive technology, or AT, helps individuals with disabilities be more independent. Assistive technology devices can help a child with a disability perform tasks that the child might not otherwise be able to perform. As in Gracie's case, her picture board helps her communicate more independently even though she is unable to speak. The following are questions and answers about obtaining assistive technology for children with disabilities.

1. *What is assistive technology?*

   Under the IDEA, assistive technology devices[69] are items and pieces of equipment that increase, maintain, or improve functional capabilities of children with disabilities. Assistive technology services[70] are broadly defined as any service that directly assists a child in the selection, acquisition, or use of an assistive technology device.

2. *What are examples of assistive technology?*

   Assistive technology can be anything that helps a child function more independently. It includes equipment or devices such as pencil grips, reaching devices, adapted toys, tape recorders, calculators, standing boards, environmental control systems, adapted keyboards, modified desks and chairs, computers, computer software that provides screen reading, text reading, and screen magnification, and alternative augmentative communication systems.

   Specific disability related assistive technology examples include:
   • providing a modified key board with enlarged keys for a child with limited fine motor skills;

   • providing a modified desk or computer table to accommodate a student in a wheelchair;

---

[69] 34 CFR § 300.5
[70] 34 CFR § 300.6

- providing computer software that reads aloud the screen (screen reader) or magnifies the screen for students with visual impairments;

- providing software that reads aloud the text for students with learning disabilities that affect their reading skills;

- providing personal digital assistants (PDA) to assist in note taking and organizing for students with disabilities that affect time management, note taking, and short term memory;

- providing reaching devices to help a student get books from a book shelf;

- providing audio books for a student with a vision impairment or other disability that affects reading skills; and

- providing a device that amplifies speech for a student with a hearing impairment.

3. *What about cochlear implants and other devices that are surgically implanted, are they considered assistive technology?*

No, in 2004 the IDEA was amended to clarify that devices that are implanted in children surgically,[71] such as cochlear implants for children with hearing impairments, are not assistive technology devices that schools must provide.

4. *Is AT always expensive?*

No, assistive technology devices range from inexpensive, low tech, items such as pencil grips, clip boards, audio books, and tape recorders, to more costly, higher tech, devices such as computers and speech synthesizers. Assistive technology can be purchased, or it can be homemade. For example, in the film *The Right Stuff*, because Chuck Yeager has broken ribs, he uses a sawed off broom stick to help him close the hatch to his plane before flying off and breaking the sound barrier. Homemade assistive technology.

---

[71] 34 CFR § 300.5

5. Who pays for the assistive technology that a child needs?

If the student needs the assistive technology in order to receive an appropriate education, then the assistive technology should be written into the IEP and the public school system must ensure the assistive technology is provided at no cost to the child's parents.

6. What is the first step in obtaining assistive technology?

A good evaluation is the key to obtaining any service for a child with a disability. Assistive technology is no exception. Evaluating a child's needs,[72] including doing a functional evaluation in the child's customary environment, is included as an assistive technology service. As in Gracie's situation, the IEP team has agreed that Gracie needs an assistive technology evaluation. Once the evaluation is completed, the IEP team will meet to design a program to provide the assistive technology that Gracie needs to receive an appropriate education.

7. Are there specific requirements regarding assistive technology in the IEP process?

Under the IDEA, assistive technology is a "special factor"[73] to be considered in the IEP process. This means that the IEP team must specifically consider whether a student with disabilities needs assistive technology. If the IEP team believes the student may need assistive technology, then the team should recommend the student's assistive technology needs be further evaluated. If the IEP team then recommends that a student needs an assistive technology device, that recommendation must be specifically written into the IEP.

---

[72] 34 CFR § 300.6
[73] 34 CFR § 300.324(a)(2)

8. *What if the school provides assistive technology, like a lap top computer, can a child use it at home as well?*

   The IEP team determines whether the child needs to use the assistive technology device at home in order to receive an appropriate public education. If the IEP team recommends home use, then the child must be allowed to take the assistive technology home.

9. *What happens if the child outgrows the device or it is damaged at school?*

   The IDEA includes as an assistive technology service maintaining, repairing, or replacing[74] the assistive technology device. So, if it is damaged or requires future modification, the school must make sure that is at no cost to the parent.

10. *Some of these devices, like augmentative communication systems, seem complicated. What if the student or the student's family doesn't know how to use the technology?*

    Also included as assistive technology services are training and technical assistance[75] in using the assistive technology device for the student, and where appropriate, the student's family and professionals such as educators, rehabilitation personnel, and employers.

11. *Where can I get more information about assistive technology?*

    There is a National Assistive Technology Technical Assistance Partnership[76] that has links to projects in every state that provide assistance in obtaining assistive technology.

Assistive technology helps children with disabilities do more things for themselves and learn in inclusive settings. Parents and educators should make sure that IEP teams explore how assistive technology can help specific children with disabilities.

---

[74] 34 CFR § 300.6
[75] 34 CFR § 300.6(f)
[76] National Assistive Technology Technical Assistance Partnership, http://www.resnaprojects.org/nattap/at/statecontacts.html

Case Seven:

Reimbursement

Blake C. v. Hawaii Department of Education, (2009) [77]

Facts of the Case

A student with autism seeks reimbursement for private school tuition. A complex set of facts indicates that the student attended public school, then private school, then public school again and in the end, moved out of state. The student's annual Individualized Educational Program (IEP) had the same Present Levels of Performance from 2005-2007. Parents indicated he was taught information and skills he already knew. Documentation showed the student made very little meaningful progress until entering the private school in 2007 where he made substantial progress. The student was never considered or evaluated for assistive technology services even though his mother raised the issue. Parents wanted tuition reimbursement and reimbursement for travel expenses. Parents did not provide any documentation or amount for travel expenses so this was not considered.

Parents claim their son made no educational progress and the Individualized Educational Program (IEP) was the same from year to year. In private school, he made substantial progress so he did have the potential to progress.

---

[77] 593 F.Supp.2d 1199 (Dist. Ct. HI, 2009)

School claims there was no need to change the Present Level of Performance. School stated the only purpose of the IEP meeting was to add ESY services. The school stated they did not conduct an assistive technology evaluation because it was not a concern brought up at the meeting.

Issue

Can parents be reimbursed for private school tuition when their student made no educational progress and was not offered assistive technology services?

Applicable Law Under IDEA

An IEP team must consider whether the child needs assistive technology devices and services.[78]

"Each public agency shall ensure that assistive technology devices or assistive technology services, or both…are made available to a child with a disability."

Circuit courts are split on the standard for a free appropriate public education. The Rowley standard is "educational benefit." The refined meaning in this circuit (9th) is "meaningful educational benefit."

---

[78] 20 U.S.C. § 1414(d)(3)(B)(v) and § 1412(a)(12)(B)(i); 34 CFR § 300.105(a)

1. What is the outcome?

_____

_____

_____

_____

2. What could the teacher have done to prevent legal involvement?

_____

_____

_____

_____

Outcome of Case Seven:

Reimbursement

Outcome: Reimbursement of approximately $100,000 for private school tuition was awarded to the parents because there was no meaningful educational benefit for the student based on his IEP.

- Since the student had the potential to make progress, the school should have been sure that measurable progress was being made over the two-year period that the student attended public school;

- Assistive technology should have been considered and brought up by the special education teacher; and

- There should have been goals on the IEP that lead to meaningful educational benefit.

Case Eight:

Principal Liability

Facts of the Case

A 14-year-old boy with severe disabilities including cerebral palsy, blindness, mental retardation, and inability to speak communicated to his mother through sign language that he was molested in the bathroom at school. The student indicated the boy was bigger than him and not in his class. The mother met with the teacher and the principal. The principal informed the mother it was unlikely this occurred but that the school would be sure it monitored the bathroom. A week later, a paraprofessional took the student to the bathroom and waited outside the open door. She left for three minutes to take a phone call. When she returned the bathroom door was closed and she could hear noises from in the bathroom. The paraprofessional went in the bathroom and found a large boy sexually molesting the student. The children were separated and the parents were informed. The victim's parents filed a complaint against the principal for failing to protect their son and for not having policies and trainings for employees regarding the prevention of sexual assaults. Complex court procedures followed. Parents desired monetary damages from the state department of education for physical pain and emotional distress. This was denied resulting in the parents filing a claim against the principal under U.S.C. § 1983. Parents believe the principal created the danger for the student by not protecting the student and by not providing training for the staff on prevention of sexual assault. The principal believes there was no reckless, intentional injury-causing action.

Issue

Can a principal be held liable for students' safety?

Applicable Law Under IDEA

A superior's lack of training for subordinate employees may be the basis of liability if the failure to train shows a deliberate indifference to the rights of the persons. Qualified immunity cannot be used by school staff when they are clearly violating a constitutional right.

1. *What is the outcome?*

   _____

   _____

   _____

   _____

2. *What could have been done to prevent legal involvement?*

   _____

   _____

   _____

   _____

Outcome of Case Eight:

Principal Liability

Outcome: The principal indirectly enhanced the danger to the student by not providing employees with policies and training for the prevention of sexual assaults. This individual action showed deliberate indifference following the mother's reporting of the first sexual abuse incident.

- The principal should have found the big boy molester before the big boy molester found the victim in the bathroom. The principal should have taken the information more seriously and followed up on it;

- The paraprofessional should have been trained to know that she should not answer the phone when a student is supposed to be monitored in the bathroom; and

- The principal should have made sure policies for protecting students were on the school website or in the school handbook.

Opening the School Door to Section 504

Brenda should have been excited. Her daughter Jessica would be starting kindergarten this fall. Jessica was smart as a whip and couldn't wait to go to school. But Jessica had diabetes. The diabetes needed managing: she needed insulin administered and her blood glucose and diet monitored.[79] When she got older, Jessica would be able to manage the diabetes herself, but right now she was just too young. Maybe Brenda could go to school with Jessica. But Brenda worked. Maybe if the school had a nurse, the nurse could help Jessica. But what if there wasn't a nurse or the nurse was too busy? Brenda knew that kids with disabilities could get special services, but Jess had an illness not a disability. She certainly didn't need special education. Was there anything Brenda could get the school to do?

Brenda called the school principal, Ms. Otero. Ms. Otero understood Brenda's concern, but said not to worry. While Jessica may not need special education, her diabetes might be a disability under a law called Section 504. The school could develop something called a Section 504 Plan. The Section 504 Plan could include a nurse, or a nurse-trained staff member, monitoring blood glucose and administering insulin. Finally, Ms. Otero said that the "Section 504 Coordinator" would call Brenda to start the ball rolling to get Jessica these services.

---

[79] American Diabetes Association, http://www.diabetes.org/living-with-diabetes/know-your-rights/

Schools and Section 504 of the Rehabilitation Act

There are three federal laws that support students with disabilities in the public schools: the Individuals with Disabilities Education Act (IDEA), the Americans with Disabilities Act (ADA), and Section 504 of the Rehabilitation Act. The first, the IDEA, requires schools to provide a free appropriate public education to students with disabilities who need special education and related services. Under the IDEA, a child must have an impairment and need special education services to be considered a child with a disability. But under the other two laws, Section 504 and the ADA, a child can have a disability without needing special education. Section 504 and the ADA protect people with disabilities from discrimination based on their disability. Regarding the public schools, these laws prohibit discrimination against students with disabilities. This means that schools must provide services to meet the individual needs of students with disabilities as adequately as the schools meet the needs of students without disabilities. These services are outlined in a Section 504 Plan. The following are questions and answers regarding Section 504 and the public schools. The ADA has the same definition of disability and the same requirements regarding public school services to students with disabilities as Section 504.

A. What is a disability under Section 504?

> A person has a disability if he has a physical or mental impairment that substantially limits a major life activity. Life activities are functions such as caring for one's self, performing manual tasks, walking, seeing, hearing, speaking, breathing, learning, and working. All children who need special education under the IDEA also have disabilities under Section 504. But a child may be determined to have a disability under Section 504 and not need special education services. For example, students, like Jessica, who have illnesses such as allergies, cancer, heart disease, high blood pressure, ulcers, kidney and liver disease, epilepsy, HIV/ AIDS, or diabetes, would be covered under Section 504. Other examples include children who have a limp, paralysis, arthritis, hearing loss, learning disabilities, attention deficit disorder, traumatic brain injuries, speech impairments, mental illness, and visual impairments.

B. How do parents get Section 504 services for their child?

Complying with Section 504 is a regular education responsibility just like complying with other laws prohibiting discrimination based on race, religion, or ethnic origin. Section 504 requires that school districts identify a "Section 504 Coordinator." Parents should contact the school administration to identify their district's 504 Coordinator.

C. How is Section 504 eligibility determined?

Parents can contact the school staff to begin the Section 504 evaluation process. First, the school will evaluate the child based upon the child's needs. Then, the evaluation information will be reviewed to determine if the student has a disability. Eligibility is decided by a group: not just one individual. The group will be people who know the child, what the evaluation information means, and how to serve students with disabilities.

D. What services are required under Section 504?

The school must provide the student a free appropriate public education. This means providing services to meet the individual needs of the student with a disability as adequately as the school meets the needs of students without disabilities. Schools are not required to lower standards for students with disabilities by changing the instructional level, content, or performance criteria. But Section 504 does require that schools provide students with disabilities an equal opportunity to demonstrate their knowledge and skills. Thus, a student who is blind or has difficulty taking tests might be entitled to a Braille copy of a test, shorter testing sessions, or extra time to take the test. But the content of the test is the same as the test provided to students without disabilities. Other examples of Section 504 services include:

• Providing a student who has cancer with a modified schedule that allows for rest and recuperation following chemotherapy;

• Providing a student who has a learning disability or visual impairment with a note-taker or tape recorder;

- Providing a student who has arthritis with a modified or adaptive physical education program;

- Providing a student with an emotional illness with an adjusted class schedule to allow time for counseling;

- Providing a student who has a physical impairment and has difficulty walking distances or climbing stairs with extra time between classes, relocated classes, and special parking.

E. What is a Section 504 Plan?

A Section 504 Plan is a plan developed by a team, including the parents, who know the student's needs and how to serve students with disabilities. The plan documents the student's disability and the services required to ensure the student has equal access to the school program. Jessica's Section 504 Plan would document that her diabetes is a disability. Her plan would include who would monitor her glucose and administer her insulin. It might also include a plan to train school staff in a basic understanding of diabetes, Jessica's diabetes related needs, how to identify medical emergencies, and who to contact in case of an emergency. Here, Jessica is just starting kindergarten, but as she gets older she may be participating in field trips, sports, or other extracurricular activities. As those needs arise, her Section 504 Plan should include managing her diabetes in those circumstances.

F. Do parents have the right to appeal or complain under Section 504?

Parents have the right to request a hearing if they disagree with how the school is providing Section 504 services. They should contact their school district or state department of education for information about that process. Parents may also file a complaint with the federal Office for Civil Rights. Information about how to file a complaint or more information about Section 504 and the ADA can be found at the Office for Civil Rights website.[80]

---

[80] U.S. Department of Education, www.ed.gov/ocr

Section 504 is not a special education law. It is a civil rights law that protects students with disabilities. A student can have a disability under Section 504 and not need special education. Jessica doesn't need special education. She just needs a plan to manage her diabetes. With that plan in place, she'll do just fine.

 XVIII

Sticks and Stones Can Break Your Bones but Words Can Break Your Heart:

Preventing Disability Harassment in School

Jeremy was in tears and Brenda's temperature had reached the boiling point. Jeremy was in seventh grade and used a wheelchair. Everything at school had been fine until the new kid transferred in. The new kid had started calling Jeremy the "crip." Jeremy could handle some kidding about his using a wheelchair, but there was a mean and ridiculing tone to the way the new kid called him "crip." At first, Brenda, being the patient and wise mother she is, had counseled Jeremy to just ignore the new kid; with time, the teasing would stop. After all, sticks and stones could break your bones, but words could never hurt you. But, a few of the other kids thought the new kid was cool and began calling Jeremy "crip" as well. It had gotten so bad that he no longer looked forward to going to school. Brenda had complained to the school principal, but his response had been that boys will be boys and Jeremy probably needed to get used to the "real world." Brenda knew that people got teased in the real world, but she expected some adult control of this behavior.

One day, the new kid placed some chairs in front of the wheelchair accessible rest room door and Jeremy wasn't able to maneuver his wheelchair into the rest room. Fortunately, one of his friends saw the predicament and moved the chairs before Jeremy wet himself.

Because of the Individuals with Disabilities Education Act, children with disabilities successfully go to school with children without disabilities. But sometimes, incidents like this one, in which students with disabilities are picked on because they have a disability, do occur. There are two federal laws, Section 504 of the Rehabilitation Act and the Americans with Disabilities

Act (ADA) that prohibit discrimination against students with disabilities. These laws require school districts to make sure that the school environment is free from abusive and intimidating behavior towards students with disabilities by other students or school staff. This kind of behavior is considered disability harassment. Here is some information to help you recognize and handle disability harassment in school:

What is disability harassment?

Disability harassment is intimidating or abusive behavior toward a student based on a disability. This behavior can create a hostile environment in the school and deny a student equal access to the school program. Harassing a student based on their disability violates Section 504 of the Rehabilitation Act and the Americans with Disabilities Act. Under these laws schools have an affirmative obligation to make sure that students are not harassed because they have a disability.

What are some examples of disability harassment?

Calling students with disabilities names, drawing pictures or writing statements, or other conduct that is physically threatening, harmful, or humiliating. For example:

- Students continually referring to a student with dyslexia as dumb;

- Students repeatedly placing classroom furniture in the way of a student who uses a wheelchair;

- A school administrator denying a student with a disability access to lunch, field trips, assemblies and extracurricular activities as punishment for the student taking time off from school because the student needed to attend therapy sessions or a medical appointment;

- Students continually taunting or belittling a student with mental retardation by mocking or intimidating the student; and

- A teacher who is belittling or criticizing a student with a disability because the student uses accommodations in class.

What should a parent do if they feel their child with a disability is being harassed?

The parent should first contact the school principal to discuss the harassment. If the harassment continues, the parent should contact the Section 504/ADA Coordinator for the school district. Section 504 and the ADA require that school districts designate an individual to coordinate the school district's compliance with these two federal laws prohibiting discrimination based on disability. The 504/ADA coordinator should be able to help the parents resolve the harassment. The 504/ADA Coordinator for a particular school district can be located by contacting the school district administration. Parents may also contact the Office for Civil Rights (OCR) within the United States Department of Education. The Office for Civil Rights is the federal agency that is responsible for enforcing Section 504 and the ADA in the public school system. Parents can obtain more information regarding the Office for Civil Rights and disability harassment, including how to file a complaint, through its website.[81]

How can schools and school staff prevent disability harassment?

School districts should have a clear policy prohibiting disability discrimination. The policy should specifically describe disability harassment and clearly state that it is unacceptable. School staff should be trained in how to recognize and handle potential disability harassment. Moreover, parents, students, teachers, and other school staff should be encouraged to discuss disability harassment and report it if it occurs.

The school district should have a clear grievance process to be used by students, parents, educators and others if they think an individual is being harassed due to his disability. The school district should widely publicize the procedures for handling disability harassment so that students, parents, school employees, and the community are aware of what it is, that it will not be tolerated, and where and how complaints involving disability harassment are handled.

---

[81] U.S. Department of Education, www.ed.gov/ocr

Finally, if the school district receives a complaint about disability harassment, the school district should make sure that it ends immediately. The school might support the student who has been harmed by providing counseling and also counsel the individual or individuals responsible for the harassment. The district should follow up to make sure the harassment is resolved or has ended.

In the last thirty years, children with disabilities have become more integrated into our public school systems. Students and teachers have learned to appreciate that everyone has differences. Sometimes, however, individuals are picked on because they are different or have special needs. Federal law requires that schools make sure that students are not picked on or harassed because they have a disability. Sticks and stones can break your bones, but words can break your heart. When those words harass a student based on the student's disability, they also break the law.

Band Director's Unilateral Decision Denying Student with a Disability Full Participation in Marching Band Violates 504

An Arizona high school student with Down Syndrome had an IEP calling for "integration with regular peers as much as possible" and participation in marching band. Thus, the student played the drum in the marching band at football games in the fall semester. Later, the marching band, including the student with a disability, went on a field trip to Disneyland. However, the band director, on her own, decided that the student would not participate in a recording session at Disneyland or march in the parade with the rest of the band. Moreover, the band director decided that the student didn't need to bring his drum and band uniform. As a result, the student was not able to participate in the band group picture taken at Disneyland.

The band director explained that she decided the student shouldn't participate in the recording session because she knew the student couldn't sight-read music. Additionally, since he tired easily he should not march in the parade. And, finally, since he wasn't marching in the parade or participating in the recording session, he didn't need to bring his uniform or drum. Thus, he was excluded from the group picture. The student's parents filed a 504 complaint with the Office for Civil Rights.

In *Marana (AZ) Unified School District*,[82] the Office for Civil Rights decided that: "The unilateral decision by the band director to deny the student participation in the activities associated with the Disneyland trip and to treat him differently from his non-disabled peers was...not

---

[82] 53 IDELR 201 (OCR June 2, 2009)

based on the individual needs of the student." Since these decisions were unilateral and not based on the individual needs of the student, the reasons behind the decisions were not legitimate and violated Section 504.

To resolve the issue, OCR entered into a Resolution Agreement with the school district that required the district to develop a district-wide "procedure to ensure that students with a disability are provided an opportunity to participate in school sponsored activities the same as non-disabled peers, or as appropriate for the individual needs of the student." Moreover, the district agreed to provide training to all of the high school staff regarding the requirements of 504 and the Americans with Disabilities Act. Finally, to help resolve the harm to the student and his family, the Resolution Agreement required that the school district reimburse the student's parents for their costs associated with the Disneyland trip or allow him to fully participate in a future trip to Disneyland.

The ADA/504 and Assistance in Toileting in Public Before School and After School Programs

Title II of the ADA requires that state and local governmental entities provide equal access to programs and services to qualified persons with disabilities. Public schools are covered by Title II and their before and after school child care programs are also covered. Section 504 of the Rehabilitation Act also requires equal access to public school services for children with disabilities including before and after school child care programs. The school must consider providing reasonable accommodations to ensure a child with a disability has equal access to the before or after school child care program.

For example, in an Office for Civil Rights (OCR) decision *Chattahoochee County (GA) School District*,[83] OCR found a school district in violation of 504 because the school district asked a preschooler's grandmother to pay for an aide to accompany the child to an after-school daycare program. The child had cerebral palsy and had difficulties walking, eating, and toileting. The school district claimed it could not afford the additional expense involved in providing the aide.

The Office for Civil Rights determined that the district had a duty to provide related aids and services unless to do so would fundamentally alter the nature of the program or create an undue burden. OCR first determined that the presence of an additional staff member to assist the child would not fundamentally alter the day care program. Then OCR determined that the district could not show that hiring an aide would create an undue hardship. The Office for

---

[83] 6 ECLPR (Early Childhood Law and Policy Reporter) 26 (OCR March 5, 2008)

Civil Rights found that the cost of an additional staff person to assist the child was only $40 to $48 a day and was not an undue financial burden. So, the school district violated 504 and Title II of the ADA when it required the grandmother to pay for an aide to assist the child with toileting. Note that in determining whether it was an undue hardship for the school district to provide the toileting assistance for the child, OCR compares the cost of the assistance to the budget for the entire school district. In that light, an accommodation would have to be very costly to be considered an undue hardship on the school district.

Protection from Retaliation

Sometimes individuals are intimidated or harassed because they are trying to enforce or help others to enforce the right to be free from disability based discrimination under Section 504 and the Americans with Disabilities Act (ADA). Both of these laws protect individuals with disabilities from discrimination. Additionally, these laws prohibit retaliation against a person with a disability (or persons who are acting on behalf of a person with a disability) for trying to enforce their rights under these civil rights laws. Individuals with disabilities and their families are often dependent on service providers such as schools and others for their services. Individuals are often reluctant to question how services are delivered because they fear they will face a reduction or termination of services as payback.

The anti-retaliation provisions of Section 504 and the ADA help allay that fear of payback so that individuals are not as afraid to enforce their rights or the rights of their family members and associates with disabilities. The anti-retaliation provisions of Section 504 and the ADA[84] are very broad. It is a violation of Section 504 and the ADA to intimidate, threaten, coerce, or discriminate against an individual who has engaged in a protected activity. Protected activities include filing a complaint, testifying, assisting in, or participating in an investigation or hearing under Section 504 or the ADA. The key elements in a complaint for retaliation are:

---

[84] 28 CFR § 35.134

1. The person making the retaliation claim engaged in a protected activity (they asserted a right, filed a complaint, testified, assisted or participated in an investigation or hearing under Section 504 or the ADA);

2. The entity that it is alleged to have retaliated knew the person engaged in a protected activity;

3. That entity took some action against the individual making the complaint and that action was at the same time that individual engaged in the protected activity; and

4. A causal connection can be reasonably inferred between the retaliatory action taken by the entity and the person engaging in the protected activity.

A good example of retaliation is the Ninth Circuit Court of Appeals case of *Settlegoode v. Portland Public Schools*.[85] In that case, Pamela Settlegood was hired by the Portland Public Schools as an adaptive physical education teacher, on a probationary basis, to teach students with disabilities in various schools within the district. She soon became concerned about how her students were treated. As an itinerant teacher, she had trouble finding a place to teach her students, she often lacked material and equipment, and the equipment that was available was inadequate and unsafe. After she complained in writing to her supervisors that her students were not getting services they were entitled to under the IDEA and Section 504, her evaluations became more negative and her probationary contract was not renewed.

Ms. Settlegood then successfully sued the school district for retaliating against her for trying to protect the rights of her students with disabilities. She was able to show that (1) she engaged in a protected activity (aggressively complaining about the lack of appropriate services and equipment for her students with disabilities); (2) the school district knew she had engaged in that activity; (3) the school district took action against her by school personnel giving her poor evaluations and not renewing her contract; and (4) it can reasonably be inferred that her poor evaluations and the non-renewal of her contract was caused by her efforts to enforce the rights of her students with disabilities.

---

[85] *Settlegoode v. Portland Public Schools*, 371 F.3d 503 (9th Cir. 2004), cert. denied, 125 S.Ct. 478 (U.S. 2004).

As noted, individuals with disabilities and their family members who depend on others for services are often reluctant to enforce their rights because they fear their services might be terminated or reduced. Anti-retaliation legislation deters agencies from retaliating against individuals who try to enforce their civil rights and helps assure individuals that they may safely pursue their rights without risking losing their services. For more information about the ADA, Section 504, protection from retaliation and how to file complaints see the Office for Civil Rights (OCR) within the Department of Education,[86] OCR within the Department of Health and Human Services,[87] and the Equal Employment Opportunity Commission.[88] Some states also have laws protecting individuals with disabilities from retaliation, so it might be helpful to check your state statutes.

---

[86] U.S. Department of Education, http://www2.ed.gov/about/offices/list/ocr/docs/howto.html

[87] U.S. Department of Health & Human Services, http://www.hhs.gov/ocr/office/file/index.html

[88] U.S. Equal Employment Opportunity Commission, http://www.eeoc.gov/employees/howtofile.cfm

Case Nine:

Section 504

Facts of the Case

Parents repeatedly asked the school district to evaluate their son for a 504 plan so he could receive accommodations. A meeting was held with school officials only, no parent attended. At the meeting, the school decided that the high school student did not qualify for a 504 plan because he was passing his classes. The next semester, the student failed a class. The principal told the mother it was too late for a 504 plan because they don't give them to eleventh grade students. The counselor was prepared to evaluate and write up the 504 plan but the principal told her not to bother since the student was failing now. Teachers indicated they were providing informal accommodations. Parents filed with the Office for Civil Rights as a violation of Section 504 of the Rehabilitation Act which prohibits discrimination on the basis of disability.

Parents stated that their son had a medical diagnosis of Attention Deficit Hyperactivity Disorder (ADHD) and struggled in school. A 504 plan would give him the accommodations he needed to succeed in school and in college.

The Principal decided, on her own, that the student could not have a 504 plan for several reasons.

Issue

Is the student entitled to a Section 504 plan?

Applicable Law Under IDEA

Section 504 regulations require that school districts provide a free appropriate public education to qualified students with disabilities.[89] A qualified student with disabilities is any person who has a physical or mental impairment which substantially limits one or more major life activities.[90] Section 504 requires that students with disabilities that substantially limit one or more life activities are fully and timely evaluated by a group of persons and that a system of procedural safeguards is in place to ensure that recipients comply with the law.[91] The recipients also must provide notice of the procedural safeguards to the public. [92]

---

[89] 34 CFR § 104.33
[90] 34 CFR § 104.3
[91] 34 CFR § 104.35
[92] 34 CFR § 104.36

1. *What is the outcome?*

    _____

    _____

    _____

    _____

2. *What could the teacher have done to prevent legal involvement?*

    _____

    _____

    _____

    _____

Outcome of Case Nine:

Section 504

Outcome: A resolution agreement was reached. The school was in violation for (1) failure to accommodate, and (2) no procedural safeguards given to parents. It can be assumed that there will be 504 training in this school.

- Post 504 procedures on the school/district website, including procedures for filing a grievance;

- A 504 plan should have been considered and/or implemented even though the student was receiving passing grades; and

- The school should have known that informal accommodations do not replace a 504 plan. The 504 plan can be used by students when they go to college.

Case Ten:

Excessive Force/Disability Harassment

Facts of the Case

A special education teacher was arrested on criminal charges of child abuse. A 12-year-old male student with severe autism was in her class for over a year. The paraprofessionals reported the teacher's actions to the vice principal. The student used pinching regularly when he wasn't able to get what he wanted. On one occasion, the student refused to do his work and pinched the teacher. She then held his hands behind his back and pushed his head onto a desk while leaning on top of him. The student's eyes bulged and his lips turned blue. A paraprofessional told her to stop and she replied, "This is my f-ing class and I'll run it the way I see fit." There were several other incidents of physical abuse. The student often wet his pants due to his developmental disabilities and his lack of toilet training. On one occasion, the teacher hit the student on the back of the head telling him, "You will not piss in my class." Another time, the teacher spanked the student after he wet his pants, leaving fingerprints on the student's butt. The teacher also verbally abused the student daily, including calling the student an "asshole" and using the F word. The student began acting aggressively outside of the classroom. The parents observed their son hitting himself on the back of the head and repeating, "You f-ing stupid." The parents claim a violation of 42 U.S.C. § 1983, the qualified immunity doctrine which could protect the teacher. Criminal charges were also filed in the state where the events occurred.

The teacher believed the use of force was appropriate. There was no constitutional violation and even if there was, teachers have qualified immunity.

The parents state that, although, there was no serious bodily injury, there was physical, mental and emotional injury. It is difficult to show psychological injury with a child who is non-verbal, and has severe disabilities but the documentation that his behavior deteriorated was clear.

Issue

Was the teacher's use of force justified?

Applicable Law Under IDEA

Teachers are immune from personal liability if the discretionary actions they take in the course of their employment do not violate a student's established constitutional rights. The 14th Amendment guarantees the right to Due Process including protection from abuse by government employees (teachers). Determining factors may include: (1) need for force, (2) amount of force, (3) extent of injury, (4) whether force was used in good faith or with malice, (5) helplessness of the student. Excessive punishment is forbidden by the 14th Amendment, specifically in schools.

1. *What is the outcome?*

    _____

    _____

    _____

    _____

2. *What could have been done to prevent legal involvement?*

    _____

    _____

    _____

    _____

Outcome of Case Ten:

Excessive Force/Disability Harassment

Outcome: Teacher did not have immunity because there was not one incident, but a pattern of abusive behavior. The teacher was sentenced to three years probation, loss of teaching license, and a ban on working with children.

- It is assumed that teachers recognize that use of excessive force violates the constitutional rights of students so avoiding such action prevents criminal charges. Clearly, the teacher in this case should not have hit her student;

- Corporal punishment should not be used when addressing the uncontrollable behavior (e.g., pinching, wetting pants) of a student with special needs. Thus, the teacher should not have spanked her student for wetting his pants; and

- Administrative action should have occurred immediately, before the abuse became a pattern.

We Can Work It Out Part I:

Using Mediation to Resolve Disputes Under the IDEA 2004

Mediation is a process in which an objective and impartial[93] third party (the mediator) works with both sides of a dispute to help them reach an agreement to resolve the dispute. Unlike a hearing officer, the mediator does not weigh evidence and resolve legal issues. Under the IDEA, the mediator's job is to help the parents and school district reach an agreement. In that process, the mediator will meet with each side to the dispute, separately or together (depending on the style of the mediator) and try to resolve disagreement.

For the mediation process to work, the participants need to be able to speak freely. Thus, the discussions that occur in mediation under the IDEA are confidential.[94] Prior to the IDEA 2004, mediation agreements resolving special education disputes were not legally binding. The agreements were voluntary and each side relied on the other's good will to comply with the agreement. Congress, however, received comments that since mediation agreements could not be legally enforced, parents and school districts were sometimes reluctant to use the process. Thus, in the IDEA 2004, Congress required that if an agreement is reached in mediation, it can be enforced in state court or a United States district court.[95]

---

[93] 34 CFR § 300.506(c)
[94] 34 CFR § 300.506(b)(6)
[95] 34 CFR § 300.506(b)(7)

Mediation can be used to resolve any special education issue, including issues that occur before a due process complaint notice[96] is filed. So, mediation can be used to resolve disagreements without requesting a due process hearing or it can be used to settle disputes after a hearing has been requested. Moreover, to encourage mediation, the IDEA requires that the State Education Agency[97] maintain a list of qualified mediators[98] and bear the cost of the mediation process.[99]

So, mediation does not cost the parents or the school districts anything other than their time. Mediation is voluntary and both parents and the school district must agree for the mediation to occur. Additionally, the State Education Agency must assure that mediation is not used to deny or delay[100] a parent's right to a due process hearing. Thus, by agreeing to mediation neither the parents nor the school district give up the right to pursue a due process hearing if the mediation is unsuccessful.

---

[96] 34 CFR § 300.506
[97] U.S. Department of Education, http://wdcrobcolp01.ed.gov/Programs/EROD/org_list. cfm?category_ID=SEA
[98] 34 CFR § 300.506(b)(3)
[99] 34 CFR § 300.506(b)(4)
[100] 34 CFR § 300.506(b)(1)

We Can Work It Out Part II:

Using the Resolution Process to Resolve Disputes Under the IDEA 2004

As yet another way to resolve disputes before a due process hearing, the IDEA 2004 added a resolution process.[101] Once a due process complaint notice is filed, the school district is required to convene a resolution meeting between the parents and the relevant members of the IEP team. The purpose of the resolution meeting is for the parents to discuss the due process complaint and give the school district an opportunity to resolve the dispute.

The relevant members of the IEP team are those members who have specific knowledge about the facts identified in the due process complaint. The parents and the school district will mutually determine which members of the IEP team are relevant. Additionally, the meeting must include a representative of the school district who has the authority to make decisions on behalf of the school district.

The meeting, however, may not include an attorney representing the school district unless the parents[102] bring an attorney to the meeting. So, the parents have an opportunity to meet with school staff without the school district's attorney being present. If parents choose to bring an attorney to the resolution meeting, then the school district may also bring its attorney.

---

[101] 34 CFR § 300.510
[102] 34 CFR § 300.510(i)

Moreover, should parents choose to be represented by an attorney at the resolution meeting, the parents may not be awarded attorneys' fees[103] for their lawyer's time attending the meeting. The resolution meeting is required unless the school district and the parents agree in writing to waive it or the two sides agree to use mediation instead. If the dispute is resolved through the resolution meeting, the parents and the school district will develop and sign a written settlement agreement. Similar to the mediation agreement, the resolution settlement agreement[104] is enforceable in state court or United States district court. But, either the parents or the school district have three business days after the agreement is signed to void,[105] or get out of, the agreement.

Finally, from the parents' perspective, the resolution session is essentially another IEP meeting but, perhaps, without the school district's attorney. On the other hand, the mediation process involves an outside person, the mediator, who can help facilitate resolving the dispute. For that reason, parents and the school district might choose to use the mediation process instead of the resolution process. Using either process will be beneficial if disputes are resolved without the need for a due process hearing.

---

[103] 34 CFR § 300.517(c)(2)
[104] 34 CFR § 300.510(d)
[105] 34 CFR § 300.510(e)

Due Process Hearing

Sometimes mediation, the resolution session, or other efforts do not resolve the dispute and parents or the school district still wish to have a Due Process hearing. In order to have a hearing, the side requesting the hearing must have filed a due process complaint notice with the other side in the hearing.

Timeline for Requesting a Hearing

The IDEA 2004 established a two-year timeline[106] for requesting a hearing. Generally, the parent or the school district must request a hearing within two years of the date the parent or district "knew or should have known" about the violation that is the basis for the hearing request. This timeline, however, will not apply to a parent if the parent was prevented from requesting a hearing because (1) the school district specifically misrepresented that it had resolved the problem, or (2) the school district withheld information from the parent that the district was required to give the parent.

Finally, the IDEA's two-year timeline will apply unless the state has its own explicit timeline for requesting a hearing. Thus, parents, advocates, and attorneys should always check their state's laws and regulations.

---

[106] 34 CFR § 300.511(e)

Qualifications of the Hearing Officer

The hearing will be heard and the dispute decided by a qualified and impartial hearing officer.[107] The hearing officer must be qualified and impartial. In order to be considered impartial, the hearing officer cannot have a personal or professional interest that conflicts with their objectivity at the hearing. Thus, the hearing officer cannot be an employee of the State Education Agency (SEA) or the Local Education Agency (LEA) that is involved in the care or education of the student or have other interests that would affect his objectivity.

To be qualified, the hearing officer must know and understand the IDEA, its regulations, and legal interpretations of the law and regulations by the courts. The hearing officer must also know how to conduct hearings and be able to make and write decisions according to standard legal practice.

Rights in the Hearing Process

Both sides to a hearing, parent and school district, have the following rights in the hearing:[108]

- the right to be accompanied and advised by a lawyer and by individuals with special knowledge or training with respect to the problems of children with disabilities;

- the right to present evidence and confront, cross examine, and compel the attendance of witnesses;

- the right to prohibit the introduction of any evidence that has not been disclosed at least five business days before the hearing;

- the right to a written, or at the option of the parents, electronic verbatim record of the hearing;

- the right to written, or at the option of the parents, electronic findings of fact and decisions.

---

[107] 34 CFR § 300.511(c)
[108] 34 CFR § 300.512

Additionally, parents have the right to have the child present at the hearing, have the hearing open to the public, and have the record of the hearing, the findings of fact, and the decision at no cost to the parents. So, parents can obtain a transcript of the hearing at no cost. This is important because if the result of the hearing is appealed, it is likely that the entity hearing the appeal will want a copy of the hearing transcript.

Timeline for the Decision

Generally, there is a 45-day timeline[109] for the hearing officer to make a decision. But the school district has 30 days[110] from the time it receives the parents' request for a hearing to try to resolve the dispute. Thus, the 45-day timeline for the hearing to be conducted and a decision issued may not begin until after that 30-day time period expires.[111] But if the parents and the school district agree in writing to waive the resolution session or agree in writing that it isn't possible to reach an agreement through mediation or the resolution session, the 45-day hearing timeline will begin the day after that written agreement is reached.

Appeal Process

Either side may appeal the hearing officer's decision. If the hearing was conducted locally by the school district or by an agency other than the State Education Agency, then the decision can be appealed to the State Education Agency.[112] In that event, the State Education Agency must conduct an impartial review of the hearing officer's decision[113] and then make its own independent decision. This is considered a two tiered hearing process. The first tier hearing is conducted by the school district and the second tier is the State Education Agency review. The second tier decision will be the final agency decision but can be appealed to state or federal district court.

Some states have a one tiered process with the State Education Agency, not the local school district, conducting the hearing. In that case, the state is not required to have an additional state level review and the State Education Agency decision will be the final agency decision.

---

[109] 34 CFR § 300.515
[110] 34 CFR § 300.510(b)
[111] 34 CFR § 300.510(c)
[112] 34 CFR § 300.514(b)
[113] 34 CFR § 300.514(b)(2)

Once the state has made its final decision (whether the state conducts the hearing or reviews an appeal of a hearing conducted by the school district) that decision can be appealed by either the parents or the school district filing a civil action (lawsuit) in state or federal district court.[114]

Concluding Thoughts Regarding Due Process Hearings

Generally, due process hearings are contentious, adversarial, costly, and unpleasant for all involved. The hearing itself is often like a trial. Attorneys for both sides present evidence, examine their witnesses, cross examine the other side's witnesses, and make oral and written legal arguments. The hearing officer presides over the hearing like a judge presides over a trial. Because the hearing is costly and unpleasant, everyone involved is usually very interested in resolving the disagreement so that a hearing can be avoided. Thus, in most cases in which a due process complaint notice is filed, the issue is settled before the hearing occurs. That is good.

But, having said that hearings are generally costly, contentious, adversarial, and unpleasant, they are sometimes very necessary. There are times in which the issues are significant and do not get resolved. In those circumstances, a due process hearing may be necessary to ensure that a student receives a free appropriate public education.

---

[114] 34 CFR § 300.516

Index

The Legal Center for People
with Disabilities   and Older People

Colorado's Protection & Advocacy System

About our organization...

The Legal Center is a nonprofit organization protecting the human, civil and legal rights of people with disabilities and older people established in 1976. As Colorado's Protection and Advocacy System, The Legal Center has authority under federal law to gain access to facilities and records in order to investigate allegations of abuse and neglect. The organization also helps people obtain state and federally funded services, such as special education, mental health services, developmental disabilities services, and vocational rehabilitation. The Legal Center specializes in civil rights and discrimination issues.

The Legal Center promotes systemic change to sustain or improve the quality of life for children and adults with disabilities and senior citizens. The Legal Center provides direct legal representation, education, advocacy and legislative analysis to promote the independence, self-determination, empowerment and community participation of its clients. Similar organizations exist in every state and territory as part of the National Disability Rights Network.

About the authors...

Dr. Jacque Phillips, Esq.

Dr. Jacque Phillips has a doctorate in Special Education (Emotional Disabilities) and a law degree. She conducts trainings for school districts, parents and attorneys on Special Education Litigation Prevention. She is an adjunct professor for the University of Northern Colorado, University of Colorado-Denver and Lehigh University in their special education departments. She also has a private law practice, the Law Office of Dr. Jacque Phillips, Esq.

Dr. Phillips was formerly a professor at the University of Hawaii and ran the special education department at Adams State College. She was the lead teacher at Platte Valley Youth Services Center when the maximum security juvenile detention facility opened. She has extensive presentations and publications at the national and international level. She taught in Burma and Kenya prior to returning to Colorado for law school.

More recently, Dr. Phillips was a legal intern for The Legal Center for People with Disabilities, the U.S. Department of Education and The Dvorchak Law Office (Juvenile Law). She studied international law in Israel and at the International Criminal Tribunal for Rwanda.

Most importantly, she is the grandmother to Sophie and Zach.

Randy Chapman, Esq.

Randy Chapman came to The Legal Center in 1977 as a Volunteer in Service to America (VISTA). He was newly graduated from law school at the University of Texas at Austin. A year later he was hired as a staff attorney. He has been the Director of Legal Services since 1980. He played a pivotal role in the development of disability law and he helped break ground in implementing special education law. His influence is reflected in Colorado statute and policy. In the developmental disabilities area, he established Human Rights Committees in legislation to review medications, behavioral programs, and ensure investigation of abuse and neglect. He added the requirement that people with developmental disabilities be represented on the boards of directors of community service organizations. He also drafted the due process language in the state statute and had significant input in the development of the Colorado Department of Education's complaint process for children in special education. He has overseen legal representation to more than 10,000 people with disabilities in Colorado and made more than 500 presentations on disability law.

In 1998 he was awarded the Martin Luther King Jr. Humanitarian Award by the Martin Luther King Jr. Colorado Holiday Commission. In 2010 the Colorado Department of Education honored him with an award for his 30 years of work supporting the parents of children with disabilities. The award was presented at the Parents Encouraging Parents or "PEP" conference, an annual conference that brings parents and professionals together to share ideas, discuss concerns, and obtain information on parenting, educating and supporting a child with a disability.

He is the author of the first and second editions of The Everyday Guide to Special Education Law, (The Legal Center 2005 and 2008), Guiá de la Ley de Educación Especial (The Legal Center 2007), The New Handbook for Special Education Rights (The Legal Center 2000), Assistive Technology: Universe of Opportunities (The Legal Center 1999), numerous articles regarding the legal rights of people with disabilities and authors RandyChapman's Ability Law Blog at randychapman.wordpress.com providing practical comments and information regarding special education, early intervention, and disability law.

He lives in Golden, Colorado, with his wife and two sons.

The Legal Center for People
with Disabilities and Older People

Colorado's Protection & Advocacy System

To order additional copies of
Preventing Litigation in Special Education Workbook
or our other publications

Online: **www.TheLegalCenter.org**

By Phone: **1-800-288-1376** or
(303) 722-0300

You may contact us by email at

Publications@TheLegalCenter.org

Or you may send us mail at

**The Legal Center
455 Sherman Street, Suite 130
Denver, CO 80203**

Quantity discount pricing is available.

Send us your comments or suggestions for future editions.

Thank you for buying this workbook!